Make Yourself Hard To Kill

~

Matteo Barbucci

AOS Publishing, 2025

Copyright © 2025

Matteo Barbucci

All rights reserved under International and Pan-American copyright conventions

ISBN: 978-1-83432-011-3

Cover Artist: Meredith Lindsay

Visit AOS Publishing's website:

www.aospublishing.com

Contents

Preface 1

Free Your Mind 7

Don't Tread on Me 13

Leave The World Behind 17

Never Complain, Never Explain 21

Never Mind 29

R.E.S.P.E.C.T. 33

Loyalty Is Thicker Than Blood 35

Word Is Bond 39

Malocchio 41

Andreia 43

Rituals 61

Linguistic Magic 69

Health Is Wealth 79

You Are What You Eat 81

God Body 87

Starve The Body, Feed The Soul 97

Sexual Transmutation 101

Third Eye Open 113

No Mud, No Lotus 119
The Art Of Dying.. 123
References 131

Preface

Once upon a time, I was caught in a relentless cycle of self-destruction. Physically exhausted, mentally tormented, and spiritually disoriented, I stumbled through life. Each step was a struggle, each breath a gasp for air in the suffocating grip of life.

My days were a haze. I tried everything and anything to numb the pain but never silenced the demons within.

I lived in fear, haunted by ghosts that shadowed my every move, sleepwalking through life and stuck in a never-ending nightmare. I questioned my sanity, standing at the edge of despair as suicidal thoughts whispered in the darkest corners of my mind.

But within the chaos, I found hope. A spark of resilience pushed me to fight against the darkness that threatened to consume me. I knew that I couldn't go on living like this, imprisoned within the walls of my own design. Something had to change. I was determined to find a way out of this nightmare.

With each passing day, I took small steps toward redemption. I embraced change and leaped into the unknown, reclaiming control over my mind, soul, and body, one day at a time.

The path to freedom was full of obstacles, and setbacks were inevitable. I faltered and failed, falling prey to old habits and destructive patterns. Yet with each fall, I rose stronger and more determined than before, refusing to let my past define my future.

As I embarked on this journey of self-mastery, I delved into the depths of my own psyche, seeking answers to the questions that haunted me. I confronted the traumas of my past, unraveling the tangled threads of my subconscious mind to reveal the roots of my pain.

In the pages of books, I found more than just words; I found maps to a thousand roads. I read with curiosity, seeking to crack the code that kept me trapped in mediocrity. Each book reminded me that freedom is not given but seized by those willing to burn the boats.

But knowledge alone wasn't enough; it demanded action, testing, proof of concept. So I stared down my fears, pushed myself into the unknown, and stood in the crossfire of my own doubts. Stepping out of my comfort zone wasn't easy; it was a leap into fire, a trial by intensity where every nerve was tested. The power to change had always been there, dormant and waiting. All it needed was my will, unflinching and relentless, to bring it alive.

Through sweat and strain, I shaped a body that could match the strength of my mind. Exercise became a ritual, a relentless pursuit of resilience and control. And proper nutrition taught me that you are what you eat, quite literally. Then I stretched into awareness, forcing myself to confront the limits of my body and bend them at will. Healing therapies patched me up after every test. In the precision of physical mastery, I found proof that strength wasn't something inherited but earned, built piece by piece.

And then, deeper still, was the spirit—wild but quiet. Meditation stripped me of pretense, laid bare the raw essence of existence, grounding me in the simplicity of the present. Fasting carved out space within, a kind of reset, a recalibration of desire and discipline. And abstinence—it was rebellion against modern indulgence, a vow of clarity in a world of excess. In these practices, I became unshakable, immune to the distractions that tried to chain me. My spirit, once scattered, was now grounded, wielded with an authority only the truly self-possessed know.

Preface

Bit by bit, I pieced together the fragments of my shattered mind, forging a new identity from the ashes of my old self, like a phoenix. I shed the shackles of doubt and fear, embracing a philosophy of integrity and authenticity that resonated deep within my soul.

Today, I stand tall and proud, a testament to true resilience. I have conquered my demons and reclaimed my life, emerging from the darkness stronger and more alive than ever before. The journey was long and tough, but it was worth it.

At the bottom of despair, I found the strength to rise. Through adversity, I forged a spirit that cannot be broken. And in the silence of my own heart, I discovered the truth that had been waiting for me all along: that the power to change lies within each and every one of us, waiting to be unleashed by the force of our will.

MIND

Free Your Mind

From the moment you were born, you were unconsciously cast in a multigenerational drama, a theatrical spectacle of indoctrination masked as societal convention. The puppet masters design the stage upon which you perform, directing a play of conformity and suppressing true original thought. You think you're making choices, but most of the time, you're just reading lines written by someone else.

Imagine this conspiracy unfolding across generations with the plot to mold minds, suppress independence, and birth a legion of obedient followers. The perpetrators? Ancient dynasties, blue bloods, Rockefellers, and Rothschilds—trillionaire heirs to legacies of decay. Their influence is woven into the fabric of our beliefs, our actions, our lives. They have inserted themselves so seamlessly into the world's systems of power that, by the time we question them, we're already too deep, enmeshed in the machinery of manipulation that's as old as civilization itself. This is the true tragedy—a cycle of control that outlives the puppet masters themselves, infecting each new generation with the same toxin of submission.

Everyone is playing their role in this global conspiracy, whether they know it or not.

Teachers whisper sweet promises of knowledge and enlightenment while subtly indoctrinating you into a system that thrives on conformity. The educational curriculum dictates what knowledge is permissible, which ideologies are acceptable, and which deviations are inadmissible.

Religion presents a set of doctrines as absolute truths, discouraging any deviation from the prescribed path: "Kneel! Surrender your soul, and paradise is yours!" But question, think for yourself, and you risk exile. Obedience is the price of salvation, and freedom is the sacrifice.

Pop culture, with its manufactured stars and heroes, isn't just entertainment—it's a modern-day brainwashing machine created to shape your beliefs and steer your desires. Each pop song, every blockbuster movie, every viral moment is designed to feed you a reality that keeps you chasing illusions. You're given idols to worship, ideas to consume, and a life script that isn't even yours. It's not entertainment—it's mind control, and you're the experiment.

Mainstream media, the propaganda machine, fabricates lies and manipulates truths for political purposes. Real journalism is suppressed and almost outlawed—narratives are crafted to serve the interests of the few, rather than illuminate the realities of the many. They work on people's emotions, pitting one against the other. With each headline, each soundbite, the lines between fact and fiction blur. As the media moguls pull the strings of perception, the pursuit of truth becomes more challenging, time-consuming, and effortful.

The food industry is slowly digging your grave by laying the groundwork for major health issues. Genetically altered foods contribute to the problem, introducing substances found to be toxic to both the environment and human health.

The medical cartel, pharmaceutical drug lords, promise healthcare in the form of quick fixes. They parade as benevolent healers but are merchants of perpetual dependence. Pills to numb the pain, vaccine shots to the veins—all packaged with a grin that conceals the hidden toll on our bodies. This corrupt network thrives on conflicts of interest, shaping healthcare for monetary gain. Physicians, bound by corporate regulations and lured by personal investments, can be swayed, leading to financially motivated treatments and care. Manipulated medical education, distorted research findings, and pharmaceutical-funded training further corrupt the system. Patients, caught in this system, will find themselves subjected to unnecessary surgeries, ineffective drugs, and biased advice. Ain't no money like dope money. We're talking big Bs—BILLION$... Forget about regulations; the regulators are bought.

Nothing that the government does is to help you. There is always a profit advantage. None of these politicians, pharmaceutical executives, or so-called "medical experts" care about you. It's always about advancing their careers or just keeping their jobs. There needs to be something in it for them, or else they wouldn't be in it. Don't be fooled! Everyone is just looking out for themselves.

Politics are the Olympics for sociopaths. Bribed mouthpieces masterfully manipulate public opinion and craft narratives that serve the interests of the elites who control them.

All politicians are full of shit. The Left is full of shit. The Right is full of shit. Everyone in between is full of shit. It's a shit show. That said, the right often shows more diversity of thought—while the left increasingly resembles an echo chamber—as per a 2023 study published in the *British Journal of Social Psychology*. [58]

But they all play their role—puppets for the elites pulling the strings. Behind closed doors, they sip champagne, toasting to a system that keeps the masses fighting over Left and Right while they tighten their grip on your soul.

Divide and conquer!

Keep everyone fighting while the true game is played behind closed doors.

PS : Not everyone is corrupted by personal greed or globalist agendas. The west stands at the edge of monumental shifts in leaderships, a turning of the tide that promises—if steered with vision—to carve a path toward brighter, bolder years ahead. But as a general rule, everything I said holds true.

***

How do you break free from this illusion? How do you resist the indoctrination and forge your own truths?

This battle is fought with the weapons of consciousness and awareness.

Our great war is a spiritual war. Stand against the sinister forces that seek to mold, manipulate, and control.

The first step on the quest for truth is to question your beliefs. Where do they come from? Are they authentic manifestations of your thoughts or implanted seeds sown by external forces?

Question not only your beliefs about the world but also your beliefs about yourself. Who are you? What is your purpose? Who do you want to be?

Question the authenticity of the narratives presented by those in positions of power.

You have a choice between the red pill, which represents an uncomfortable truth, and the blue pill, which represents blissful ignorance.

Question your reality and challenge the simulated world imposed upon you.

The journey toward making your own ideas does not come without its challenges. It requires a departure from the safety of the familiar and a willingness to embrace the uncertainty of the unknown.

The richness of human experience lies in the acceptance of both the joys and the pains. Make your own ideas about the value of every experience, even the ones that bring you discomfort.

Don't Tread on Me

History is stained with the blood of those who dared to defy the shackles of oppression.

The essence of our existence is on the line. Freedom is going extinct.

The concept of freedom hangs on the precipice of extinction, assaulted by forces unseen but profoundly felt.

Freedom, the light that guided our predecessors through the darkest nights, might flicker and fade.

Freedom is not inherited but something that demands eternal vigilance, the relentless fight of each generation.

Freedom is not a birthright granted to you by fate. It is a choice—a bold decision that breaks free from the constraints of tyranny and conformity. With this choice comes the responsibility to guard and preserve it.

Born into a culture sculpted by hands that bled for the ideals we now hold, we stand on the shoulders of rebels, pioneers, and forgotten heroes.

In this digital age, privacy is a memory of a lost time. We willingly surrender pieces of our freedom for the illusion of security, blissfully unaware that the more we relinquish, the less remains.

In a world drowning in an overflow of information, the truth becomes an elusive entity. Mainstream media propaganda is distorts reality and blurs the lines between fact and fiction.

Censorship, masked as the righteous pursuit of eliminating disinformation, misinformation, or malformation, creeps in, silencing opposing voices and turning the marketplace of ideas into a sanitized echo chamber. The battleground is not only physical but mental, in the minds of the masses.

To watch passively as tyranny creeps in is to be complicit. The air of complacency carries the foul odor of surrender. Embrace the fear that accompanies the rejection of submission.

Peel back the layers, expose the bullshit, and confront the distorted narratives.

The assault on freedom, insidious and relentless, demands a response that transcends the conventional. It calls for the unruly and defiant, the free thinkers, and the rebellious.

The choice is yours—surrender to conformity or unleash the full fury of the rebellious spirit in defence of freedom. The price of liberty, as paid by the generations before us, demands nothing less than your firm commitment.

Defend your freedom!

***

There is a war for your soul. It's not just about flesh and bones, it's about the essence of who you are, who you've been, and who you could still become. It's deeper than just the physical.

DO YOU UNDERSTAND?

The struggle for your soul is realer than ever.

What does it mean to die spiritually? It included betraying your own values, selling out your principles, and letting fear and aggression run your life. It's a soulless existence.

The soul has to suffer first to know paradise. It's a universal law—endure the storm to find eternal peace. If you take the easy way out, conform to the system, and tolerate weakness, you will know hell.

Suffering is universal.

Suffering isn't the enemy; it's training for your mind, body, and soul. It toughens you up, makes you resilient.

Look into yourself—know yourself.

We're all flawed, full of love and hate, complex beings on this beautiful blue planet. Life is rare, and we are not going to make it out alive.

Leave The World Behind

It is through action, not words, that the true character of a person or a society is revealed.

Society is turning soft. People are weak, gripped by fear, suppressed in political correctness, entrapped in entitlement, hypersensitive, perpetually immature, and prisoners of convenience.

Hard times create strong men, strong men create good times, good times create weak men, and weak men create hard times.

Wokism is a fanatic ideology, dreamy utopias, and an appetite for control.

Conformity, suppression of opposition, and the pursuit of an ever-elusive utopia... It sounds like communism to me.

Just like the foot soldiers of the past cultural revolutions, the woke "warriors" are out to cancel anyone who doesn't get in line, all in the name of moral righteousness. Isn't it ironic, preaching inclusivity while kicking out those who think differently?

Words are turned into weapons for ideological warfare.

Chaos often tags along with radical shake-ups.

You have to rebel against this societal metamorphosis. Put up a middle finger at anyone encouraging this shit. The weak-minded, dependent on external crutches, are the real problem.

Wokism forces its influence over the collective consciousness, shaping narratives and manipulating perceptions. It promotes a climate of fear and fosters a culture of weak behaviors.

Everything's been compromised, but the ones responsible for the degeneration of our culture are the CEOs, tech moguls, influencers, educators, doctors, scientists, journalists, and politicians. They have fallen prey to the clutches of cowardice. The refusal to confront truth, the lack of spine to draw a line, the fear of financial repercussions or damaging labels—this is what got us here.

If cowardice is the anchor dragging us deeper into this mess, the only lifeline is dependent on courage and non-compliance.

Courage becomes the antidote, the shot of adrenaline in the face of a society that is sleepwalking to its death.

The path out demands a revival of courage and non-compliance. You have to fight—not with violence, but with resilience against the woke matrix that manipulates minds and exploits fears.

Act with courage and make your own destiny. Stop being a poor old victim. Empower yourself. Take control of your own life—because if you don't, someone else will.

The path ahead isn't clear, but in rebellion, we see a new dawn on the horizon. The woke monster, with its tentacles of fear and manipulation, can be dismantled by the collective will to stand firm and tall. We find eternal truths in history. Courage, when embraced collectively, becomes an unstoppable force.

The fight is not against each other but against the forces that seek to extinguish the flame of courage. The obstacles we face—the erosion of free speech, globalist propaganda, institutional and cultural decay—are the very challenges that, when confronted with courage and non-compliance, become the catalysts for societal transformation.

Wake the fuck up! Compliance is for slaves—a cage for the spirit, locking you in someone else's blueprint… cast off the chains of fear, and embrace the mantle of courage. Don't resign, defy.

Now is the time for courage. Now is the time for non-compliance. Now is the time to cast off the shackles of fear and manipulation.

Pursue self-reliance and personal growth relentlessly.

Kill your inner resistance—that's what separates the warriors from the weak.

Reject false securities and embrace challenges that forge strength, resilience, and true self-reliance.

Society is fooled into submission by promises disguised in moral justice. Free money, free healthcare, free housing—ain't nothing free in this world! If "their" generosity comes with strings, it's not a gift—it's a leash.

Don't let "them" dim your light.

Don't let "them" kill your ambition.

"They" want you to reject personal responsibility and embrace victimhood, but relying on others kills personal strength.

Don't allow yourself to get caught in relying on anything outside of yourself, giving up control over your own life. You have to focus on what you can handle—the internal choices, actions, and mindset—instead of getting down on your knees.

DO NOT SURRENDER to softness, to fear, and to entitlement—the ones who do are already dead. Look for truth, question the narrative, break free from the shackles of convenience, and confront the discomfort of self-reliance.

You want an authentic life? Reject dependency! Nobody owes you shit.

You're not entitled to a good life.

Be self-reliant, resilient, and have the audacity to do your own work.

Wake the fuck up! Question your beliefs, reject manipulative tactics, and forge your own path.

True fulfillment lies beyond the illusions of convenience and dependency.

Create value and do shit that matters.

Life is not easy. But easy is for losers. You're not a loser!

Never Complain, Never Explain

Resist the temptation to defend yourself or make excuses. Take full responsibility for your life, your actions, and your results.

It's not about what happens to you, but what you do with what happens to you—how you react to it.

***

When you dance with the world, you must define your own rhythm. Don't wait for the crowd to guide you—dominate the floor and make 'em move to your grooves.

Some will join and dance with you, while others will just watch. But none of that matters. You're not here to entertain; you're here to proclaim.

It's much better to be authentic and make a bad impression than to be fake, trying hard to make a good impression. Even if people dislike you, they will at least respect you for being unapologetically real. But the moment you bend to fit others' expectations, you lose the essence of yourself. And people see right through that.

Confidence follows self-respect. You don't need to explain yourself!

If people doubt you, then prove them wrong by doing it. Take action!

Show them that you're in control, and you know what you're doing. Walk with swagger—head high, shoulders back, and chest out!

Keep in mind that it's possible most people won't get it—your friends and family, your girlfriend or boyfriend. "Who do you think you are?"—type of shit. But don't worry about them! Don't waste any time or energy explaining yourself. Most won't resonate with your frequency. Accept the disconnect.

When you go against the narrative, you should expect resistance. Einstein wisely said, "Great spirits have always encountered violent opposition from mediocre minds. The mediocre mind is incapable of understanding the man who refuses to bow blindly to conventional prejudices and chooses instead to express his opinions courageously and honestly."

Have faith in yourself. Focus on yourself first.

Stop worrying about what people think. Trust me, they don't do much thinking. Be too busy to worry.

Resist the temptation to defend yourself or make excuses.

Let your actions speak louder than your words. Dance to the rhythm of your own existence, free from the need for external validation.

***

This world is relentless in its attempts to define you, box you in, and confine you. Authenticity is almost heroic. Where society fights for influence, your role is not to follow but to lead. It doesn't matter if you're at the front of the pack; what matters is that you're at the front of yourself.

Trust yourself! That's true confidence, to trust your thoughts and ideas. To move forward even when your actions are doubted or questioned. To move forward even when you might doubt or question yourself.

Never complain! The only thing that it accomplishes is the deterioration of your confidence and attraction of negative consequences. Trust the process, sidestep the noise, and focus on the core.

When you're confident, you don't feel the need to justify your actions. When you trust yourself, there's no need for external validation; explanations become insignificant. If you fold, you give up the very confidence they aim to test.

What do you think you're doing when you bend over backyards, explaining yourself to everyone, trying to justify your choices?

You're basically telling yourself, and everyone else, that you don't trust yourself.

The act of explaining reveals a lack of confidence in your choices, creations, and principles. To explain is to give up power, validate the critic's importance, and descend to their level. Let your work stand on its own, confident in its integrity and purpose.

Excuses are for the weak, the scared, the ones who can't face the harsh reality staring back at them in the mirror. It's a playground move, something a kid does when he's caught with his hand in the cookie jar.

You know why you make excuses? Fear! Fear of looking in the mirror and admitting that you're not living up to your own fucking potential. You're too soft, unwilling to roll up your sleeves and get your hands dirty. Sacrifice? That's a foreign concept to your lazy ass!

Excuses are for babies who haven't learned the first lesson of life—personal responsibility. Excuses are a poison that seeps into your veins and rots your core.

Saying sorry, although well meaning, is just an empty word implying you feel bad for what you've done. A weak-ass attempt to offset the mess you've made.

Mistakes happen; we're all human. But don't you dare cry out those empty apologies. Say it won't happen again, and by god, make sure it doesn't. Own your shit! Take accountability for what you've done, because if you don't, you're paving your own road to hell, one excuse at a time. Satan will welcome you with open arms.

The road to hell? It's not lined with good intentions! It's built by the spineless souls who refuse to own up to their choices. You might think you're on the righteous path, but are you really? You can play mental gymnastics all day, but deep down, you know the truth. It's time to cut it, face the music, and take responsibility for your life.

Stand steady by your convictions; have unshakable faith in your aspirations.

Refuse entry to doubt or fear, for those who cast shadows of negativity often submit to unfulfilled potentials and are desperate to project their misery onto you.

Don't ever lower yourself so that others won't feel insecure around you.

The Poisonous Well

Understanding when to talk and when to stay quiet is maturity.

Never Complain, Never Explain

Complaining does nothing but get you dirty. That's why it's called taking shit. You can't dish out dirt without getting some on yourself.

Complaining without purpose serves only to elevate the complainer's status, a game best left unplayed.

You might find some kind of peace in it... complaining about life's inconveniences—after all, it's your own fucking right to vent. But let me tell you something: complaining is a toxic, slow-acting poison that corrodes the very essence of your existence.

First off, let's talk about energy. Complaining is an energy vampire, sucking the life force out of you. You pour your precious vitality into venting about your partner, your job, politics, people with different opinions, the fucking weather, your boss, and what do you get in return? A brief moment of emotional release without any constructive impact, followed by an insidious drain on your spirit. It's a rigged game, and you're the sucker at the table.

Clean up your own room before you criticize the world. It's easy to point the finger at others, but different when the finger points back at you. That requires a raw honesty, an acknowledgment of your deeds, and a willingness to shoulder the weight of your existence. It demands you to step up, be an active player in society, not a sideline spectator. It commands self-awareness.

Complaints are like a contagious virus, spreading rapidly and infecting those around you. You think you're just sharing a harmless opinion, but you're really unleashing a plague upon the unsuspecting souls around you. Misery loves company, they say!

Complaining rewires your brain, turning you into a perpetual victim of circumstance. Your default setting becomes one of dissatisfaction, a never-ending loop of grievances that blinds you to the beauty flickering in the periphery.

You're a loser when you toss blame on others. It's easy to go through life as a loser, blaming anyone but yourself. So, by all means, keep at it. Play the victim, point your finger at the world, but never at yourself. It's always everybody else's fault, but never yours.

But let's get real here, how much longer can you keep this up? Someday you'll realize you fucked up.

One day... someday! But what about today?

Take a close look at yourself.

Take a long look at yourself.

Take a deep look at yourself.

Now complain about yourself. Let it all come down. It's all on you. Accept it!

Then, forgive yourself. Despite the mess in your life being your own doing, you did the best with the person you were at that moment. You couldn't have done any better or worse.

Instead of moaning and groaning about your misfortunes, embrace the chaos. Life is unpredictable, and complaining won't change it. Learn to love the madness, find humor in the absurdity, and let go of the need to control every fucking little thing.

You can be dealt a royal flush and somehow manage to fuck it up. On the flip side, you can start with a lousy hand and still win—if you can convince yourself you can despite your bad luck.

Life happens, shit happens, but... It's not about the hand you're dealt; it's about the moves you make with the cards, how you play with the twists of fate, how you defy the odds.

The world does not need to bow to anyone's wishes. The world does not exist to meet your expectations. It encourages those willing to go elsewhere, or better yet, forge a path of their own liking.

Complaining is poverty
Gratitude is riches

Fortress Of Self

The world is out to get you!

Corporations are wrestling for your attention. Governments demand your oppression. Family and friends beg for donations.

Boundaries are the fortress you build around your mind, defending it from the relentless influence of the world outside.

Just like a castle needs strong walls to repel enemy forces, your mind needs defence from invading ideas.

You know your path better than anyone else. You know who you are and where you stand. So fuck 'em! They're not in your shoes, not walking the same path. So why the hell would you place their opinion over yours?

I only take advice from someone I'm willing to trade places with.

There it is! If you're not someone I look up to, if you're not someone who inspires me, or someone I want to emulate, then why should I heed your advice?

Listen, I'm all for fresh perspectives—keep an open mind, but not so open your brains fall out. Trust your inner compass above all else, and let it guide you through the noise.

Deep down, you know the truth. Deep down, you know what to do.

People, weighted down by doubts and unfulfilled dreams, will dump their baggage on you. Without firm boundaries, you let anyone and everyone mess with your confidence. If you're not rooted in your purpose, you'll fall like a tree without roots.

As you ascend in life, your friends, family, colleagues—everyone with a cheap opinion—will crawl out of their hole to tell you what they think. Resist the urge to explain!

Focus on yourself! If someone doesn't get you, it's not your job to make them.

I'm not telling you to be an asshole! I'm telling you to know what matters—your goals, values and purpose. That's your compass guiding you. You're the captain of your soul, sailing through life's ocean. Let your truth steer you. You don't ask crew members who have never been where your going for directions! You chart the course. Take pride in your ship. Trust your ability to navigate with conviction towards your treasure—your growth and evolution.

Never Mind

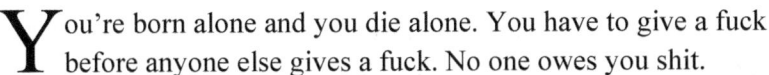

You're born alone and you die alone. You have to give a fuck before anyone else gives a fuck. No one owes you shit.

Fuck what they say. Haters are gonna hate. There is no such thing as bad publicity.

There's only one thing in the world worse than being talked about, and that is not being talked about.

In the end, the only opinion of you that truly matters is your own.

People will judge you based on their own frame of references—their emotions, beliefs and values. It's never about you, but always about them. They are really using you as a sound board. They project their current state onto you. You trigger them with your confidence and competence. They need to feed themselves excuses to rest easy at night—so you're the bad guy.

What's it to you? You cannot force people into liking you, so accept it! Who gives a fuck!

When you have real confidence, you have no reason to feel insecure. If you do, then chances are, you are not so confident.

Figuring out confidence is like solving a million piece double sided puzzle.

On the surface, it's easy to feel like confidence is reserved for the lucky & privileged. A select few who proudly display their successes while the many less fortunate remain in the shadows of their perceived inadequacies. But it's deeper than that.

Possession of external riches doesn't guarantee an internal reservoir of confidence. Au contraire, it leaves you constantly chasing for more of the thing. Billionaires second-guess their wealth, models question their appearance, and celebrities doubt their popularity.

Confidence comes from inside, not outside. It rests in the subjective realm of self-perception.

Confidence embodies the conviction of lacking nothing.

You gotta shift your perspective. It's not about believing you have everything, but about embracing what you lack. Comfort in failure unlocks real confidence.

The road to positivity passes through the valleys of negativity. Acceptance of failure doesn't define your worth but is a stepping stone to enlightenment—a gateway to fearless action, authentic engagement, and unconditioned love.

Confidence, stripped of its illusions, emerges not from the pursuit of success but from the acceptance of failure as an integral part of the human experience.

It's the puzzle piece recognizing its place in the overall picture, understanding its importance in completing the whole. It's the artist embracing the strokes of imperfection on the canvas, realizing they add depth to the masterpiece.

Don't try to find a process around your insecurities. Address 'em directly, and correct 'em immediately!

It won't be easy, but you'll come out of it better than before, because you came from nothing; you started from the bottom.

Don't listen to the nonbelievers. They will try to put you down. They will try to dim your light. They will try, but you are strong and bright. You will stand firm like an unmovable mountain. You will shine bright like a diamond.

FUCK WHAT THEY THINK!

You only have so many fucks to give. Don't throw them away on what people think of you.

Criticism will cripple you—don't allow them to handicap you.

The secret is to accept yourself fully where you are right now. Recognize your weaknesses and failures, but don't dwell in them—see through them! There is a light at the end of the tunnel. But you must be willing to walk through darkness to reach it.

Break free from the chains of external validation.

Your self-worth cannot be dependent on anything outside of yourself. Recognize that your opinion of yourself is the only one that truly matters.

We live in a time of hyper-connectivity, where social media amplifies the noise of external opinions. The pursuit of external validation often leaves you entangled in a paradoxical trap—a never-ending chase for approval that ironically erodes your sense of self. The more you seek validation from others, the more you lose control of your own story.

The reality is that the opinions of others are shaped by their own perspectives. To base your self-worth on such shaky grounds is to build a house of cards destined to crumble.

The key lies not in complete apathy but in choosing what truly matters. External opinions, often fueled by societal expectations and endless comparisons, need a critical filter for your attention.

To live a life true to yourself, to honor your values, and to pursue your passions unburdened by the weight of others' opinions is the essence of authenticity.

Cultivate a self-opinion that comes from a place of authenticity and self-awareness. The only opinion that matters is the one you hold of yourself—an opinion that transcends the transient judgments of the external world and shapes a narrative that resonates with the authenticity of your being.

Never mind the naysayers, the nonbelievers, the haters.

R.E.S.P.E.C.T.

Too many men walk around without a shred of self-respect, let alone the ability to command it from others. This is not just about poor eye contact or a limp handshake—it's about the confidence they're lacking, the refusal to step up and demand more from life. It's about missing out on promotions, opportunities, and relationships because they are invisible, even to themselves.

How you treat yourself teaches others exactly how to treat you. If you walk with your head down, if you let insecurities run you down, you're letting the world see you as unworthy of respect. But hold your head high, know your worth, and the world will start to take notice.

Respect is earned, not given.

Respect is not something you hand out like candy on Halloween. It is earned through blood, sweat, and tears. You have to climb your way up that ladder. Through integrity, action, and high standards, you communicate your expectations to yourself and the world. Step by step, leave a mark that can't be ignored.

Respect is not about titles or fancy suits. It's about character, integrity, and grit. It's about standing tall in the face of adversity, facing your demons head-on, and emerging victorious on the other side. It's about owning your mistakes, learning from them, and coming back stronger than ever. That's the kind of respect worth its weight in gold.

But here's the thing: respect is not a one-way street. It's a give-and-take where both sides have to earn their stripes. You want to be respected? You have to show respect, too. It's about treating others the way you want to be treated, lending a helping hand, and lifting each other up when times get tough. And if someone refuses to respect you after all that, cut them loose. Whether it's a boss, a romantic partner, a friend, or a family member, some people simply won't change, and it's on you to make the decision to walk away. Respect isn't something you beg for. It's something you demand through presence, action, and absolute self-respect.

Respect is a grind, a relentless pursuit of excellence in everything you do. It's about showing up, day in, day out, and giving it your all, even when the odds are stacked against you. It's about staying true to yourself, your values, your vision, no matter what the world throws at you.

When you earn respect, when you truly command it, ain't nobody gonna mess with you. You become unstoppable, untouchable, a true badass in every sense of the word.

Earn that respect. Work for it, fight for it, bleed for it if you have to. Because once you've earned it, once you've carved out your place in this world, nobody will dare question your worth.

Respect is the ultimate badge of honor in a world hungry for authenticity.

Loyalty Is Thicker Than Blood

Everybody from day one ain't your A1...

Blood might be thicker than water, but loyalty is thicker. Without it, family's just a bunch of strangers sharing a last name. You have to show up, day in and day out. Commitment, loyalty, trust—those are the bricks that build the fortress.

It's the chosen connections that have any real significance. You didn't ask to be put into this world. Like I said... respect is earned, not given. Your title doesn't mean anything. What really matters is what you do and how you do it. Can your people count on you or not? Are you giving and generous or do your actions come with a hidden price tag? Are you real or are you fake? Do you say things to my face or do you talk behind my back?

People tend to value convenience over commitment, but loyalty is the foundation of every relationship—without it, nothing holds up. The real ones will stand with you through the ups and downs of life. Chosen bonds can outshine the coercive nature of blood ties, where familial obligations can be used as emotional blackmail.

Loyalty, when invested wisely, becomes the glue that holds relationships together.

Relationships are like delicate flowers. They're the lifelines connecting you to others, shaping your experiences, and defining who you are. You have to water them, nurture them, or they die. It's a two-way street. You give, you take, you fight, you forgive. That's how you keep that flame burning bright.

Think about it like this: you plant a seed, you have to water it, give it sunlight, maybe even talk to it a little to help it grow. Relationships are the same. You have to invest time, energy, and heart into them if you want them to flourish. You have to listen, communicate, understand, and compromise. It's a dance, a delicate balancing act where both partners have to be in sync, moving together to the rhythm of mutual respect and understanding.

But here's where things get really interesting: neglect. If you stop watering that plant, it shrivels up and dies. The same goes for relationships. If you stop putting in the effort, the love, the attention —they wither away faster than a snowflake in hell. Resentment creeps in, misunderstandings fester, and before you know it, you're left with nothing but ashes where a beautiful bond once stood tall.

So how do you avoid this tragic demise? Simple—you keep nurturing. You keep showing up, day in, day out. You keep investing in the little moments, the shared laughs, the heartfelt conversations. You keep being there for each other, through thick and thin, rain or shine. That's how you keep the flame burning bright, how you keep the bonds of connection alive and thriving.

The strength of any relationship lies in commitment and understanding. It's about creating a space where individuals can be their authentic selves, free from judgment and manipulation.

Nourishing relationships involves reciprocity, communication, and a shared dedication to each other's well-being.

Relationships are what make the highs sweeter and the lows bearable. They're the glue that holds us together in a world hell-bent on tearing us apart.

So cherish 'em, nurture 'em, and watch 'em bloom into something truly beautiful. Trust me, it's worth every damn second.

But let's get real. We come into this world alone, and we come out alone. It's a solo journey, filled with highs, lows, and everything in between. But loyalty is the one thing that sticks with you through it all. It's the anchor in the storm, the North Star guiding you home.

So, respect? Earn it. Relationships? Nurture 'em. Family? Commit.

But never forget... You are born alone and you die alone.

Word Is Bond

Word is bond!

Your word is the currency of trust. Honoring that word… that's a testament to sincerity that commands respect.

Staying true to your word isn't just about keeping your promises; it's about living what you speak. In a world where words can be as empty as the echoes in an abandoned building, actions speak louder than anything your mouth can utter.

We all have friends who talk the talk but can't walk the walk. They're all about promises, but when it's time to ride, they hide. Staying true to your word is about authenticity, about living what you preach. It's about being the same person in the spotlight and in the shadows.

It's about being real with others and being real with yourself. It's about looking in the mirror and knowing that the person staring back ain't playing a role. Your word is your script, and every action is a scene. But this is real life, there's no do overs. Stay true to that script, 'cause when the curtains fall, you want to make sure you played your part right.

Intuition is your compass, pointing you to your truth when the world's trying to throw you off course. When you're at a crossroad, it's that feeling deep down that tells you which way to turn. It's the sixth sense of survival when the odds are stacked against you.

You have to keep it real; honesty fuels your instincts. If you deceive yourself, you corrupt the foundation of your existence.

Truth hurts. Most of those things you feed yourself are illusions— excuses, rationalizations, twisted versions of reality.

Stop lying to yourself! It makes you weak.

Stand firm next to your beliefs and boundaries, unaffected by external noise or your ever-changing moods. There is no room for excuses, and your emotions don't get a vote on whether you get things done.

You get conquered in those small, seemingly inconspicuous surrenders, each one slowly killing the core of who you truly are. It's not like you wake up one morning and decide to be a little bitch. No, it's a gradual, step-by-step kind of thing. It eats away at your determination—it eats away at your self-discipline.

It ain't easy in these mean streets. All you have are your instincts. They are what will keep you alive when the world tries to kill you.

Be real with yourself! Kill the doubts, the haters, the whispers of failure.

When I was down and out, when the world tried to bury me, something inside me told me to rise. It told me to keep it real, keep fighting for what I believed in, and keep moving forward.

Be a man of your word when the world wants to turn you into a walking contradiction.

When they try to silence you, turn up the volume. When they throw shade, let the light shine bright.

Malocchio

If you're going to tell people about your plans and aspirations, make sure you're confiding in the right people. You need people who will lift you up, not those who will drag you down.

When you lay it all out for those whose opinions actually matter, you add a whole new level of accountability, a layer of urgency, a fire under your ass that makes you hustle. You want to impress them—make 'em proud. You don't want to look like an idiot when you don't deliver.

But be careful, though! Don't go running your mouth to just anyone. Be discerning—watch the crowd you're in.

Your inner circle, your family, your ride-or-dies, they're not always the best sounding boards for your ambitions. They'll either be green-eyed monsters or downright confused about why you're shooting for the stars.

See, when working on becoming the best version of yourself, you're holding up a mirror to their own screw-ups and shortcomings. It might light a fire under their asses, but it could also attract bad energy, *the malocchio*, the evil eye. It's a twisted paradox—they want the best for you, but deep down, they don't want to lose the version of you that they've got lodged in their heads. The brain is tricky, clinging to survival instincts and all.

And then there's the Mr. Me Toos. They're not there to celebrate you—they're there to mirror you. These are the ones who nod along, who clap the loudest, but they're not impressed; they're opportunistic, waiting to ride your wave.

They don't just imitate—they infiltrate. These people aren't just trying to steal your style; they're going for your position. And if you're not careful, they'll use your momentum to throw themselves ahead, leaving you wondering how you got played.

Stay sharp. Guard your blueprint, your secrets, your spark. Protect your vision and your value. Know the difference between builders and takers—because you're not here to be anyone's ladder.

Watch who's circling close, and ask yourself: are they allies or parasites?

Careful who you vent to; vents connect to other rooms.

Open up to people who'll call you out when you slack, not the ones looking to pull you back.

Your friends and family? Love 'em, cherish 'em, but please…

SHUT THE FUCK UP! Don't seek validation.

Beware of the false dopamine hit you get when you talk about your goals.

Talk? It's cheap as hell. Action? That's the way. Walk the walk, and let the results do the talk.

Andreia

In a time before nuclear warheads, combat drones, and automatic machine guns, all killing was done hand-to-hand. You had to get up close and personal to execute your enemy—so close that you risked dying by your enemy's sword. The Greeks had a word for this virtuous ideal: *andreia*—where actions are valued as highly as rewards.

It's the antidote for weak spirits, lazy habits, and the excess pleasures that leave you lost—a push toward purpose and passion.

Face your own flaws—fight the demons that cling to your soul. This is a struggle against your ignorance, a fight for inner freedom.

Fueled by self-directed, constructive anger, every challenge becomes an opportunity, every setback a chance to rise stronger than before.

It's the fine line between cowardice and recklessness. It's not about brute strength but about finding the perfect balance of virtues through calculated moves.

Don't judge your results; judge your actions.

The more you sweat in peacetime, the less you bleed during war.

Fortune favors the bold.

Take calculated action, but don't calculate yourself out of action. Know enough to understand the situation, but not too much to lose to the situation.

Blood and Virtue

The vibe outside is soulless. Society is vibrating at a low frequency.

It's a cultural trip. We're drowning in too much stimulation, losing trust in everyone and everything. Real values are absent…

There's an abundance of lifestyle choices out there, and Instagram's got 'em all. We're drowning in recycled stories, and it feels like every idea worth having has already been had. Every word worth saying has been said. Can't even have a strong opinion without someone saying it's old news. Choosing a path, finding purpose? That's like trying to catch smoke with your bare hands.

So what are you going to do? Zone out on Netflix, get lost on sports statistics, or turn politics into some soap opera shit. Escaping the real issues, you know?

Getting out of this chaos, this meaninglessness on a big scale, it's like trying to make your way through a maze in the dark.

But there's a silver lining—action.

We forgot what it means to act, to take the right steps. It's not about floating around or pretending to be busy—it's about doing the real work.

To get back to the grind, you have to start with what seems like non-action—meditation. Think about what action really is, how it plays out in your life. It's not just about throwing punches; it's the subtle moves, too. Imagination, reflection, waiting—those are the real power moves. You can be doing a million things that don't mean anything.

Action isn't just about hitting goals; it's the key to finding that meaning and purpose we all crave. It's the back door to all those philosophies and religions promising some higher plane. When you're in that zone, you don't even notice the messed-up parts of our world. As the chaos settles down, the news fades into the background. It's the cure. The antidote to our chaos. Action.

When I say "action", I mean the "right action".

Right actions aren't some wishy-washy thing; they're bold, deliberate moves. They're like catching that flow, getting all focused and mindful. Virtuous—these moves bring you closer to reality, make your wildest imaginations come to life.

Now action, on the other hand, is like hunting for the next life hack to trick yourself into thinking you're productive. Right action? That's rolling up your sleeves and getting down to business.

Action is eating cheap fast food; right action is fueling up with quality proteins and organic greens.

Action is going to the gym whenever you feel like it, to chit chat and take pictures; right action is working out with consistency, proper form, and maximum effort.

Action is working a nine to five with no end goal in mind; right action is setting achievable goals and working on them day in day out, without any excuses.

Action is killing time mindlessly scrolling through social media; right action is reading a book.

Action is playing video games; right action is playing the game of life.

Action is getting dressed; right action is getting dressed to impress.

Action is complaining about problems; right action is finding solutions.

Right actions are not always these big moves. They can be small, like walking. But it's not just walking; it's walking with your head high and shoulders back and chest out, with confidence and swagger. That's right action—the difference between going through the motions and doing them with purpose.

Philosophy isn't just about pondering the meaning of life; it's about turning those deep thoughts into real actions.

True philosophers, the real ones, they're not floating in some abstract realm. They're hooked up to reality. Theories are worthless if they're not guiding your actions.

Virtue is just a pretty word unless it shapes how you move.

The real test? Putting theories into action. Take a step, feel the theory, get a grip on what was really meant. You're not going to know if it works for you until you're knee-deep in it. That's the only understanding that matters.

***

Now, sitting on your hands and doing nada? It's expensive. Inaction's a slow poison. You might not feel the pain right away, but it's rotting your soul.

Inaction breeds death.

You are scared of the wrong things and completely unafraid of the truly terrifying. That's why you do nothing.

You're not "waiting to live", you're waiting to act. That frustration, that tiredness? It's because you're stuck in the comfort zone and you're not doing anything that fulfills your soul. You have to push through the fear, the unknown, and then push some more. Commit to action, and it's not a one-time thing—it's a lifetime hustle.

You can't predict what life throws at you, but you know how you're going to act. Be prepared, train yourself for the unexpected.

Action is messy, it's creation in all its chaos. Life isn't always clean and steady. Honest action might confuse you and those around you at first, but it straightens your spine. You don't fear what others fear, you don't regret like they do.

Scars are lessons. They make you! There's no way around it… you have to ditch the training wheels and embrace the falls, the pain, and do it again.

Kick off before you think you're ready. Get in the mud and get dirty.

Experience is where the real action is. Theory becomes reality through practice.

***

Motivation is cheap! It'll get you hyped for a little moment, but it won't stick around when things get tough.

Motivation is up and down. It's ultimately unreliable.

How do you stay in the game? Action. Real power. Oh, you're tired, you're scared, you're feeling overwhelmed? Poor you. Shut the fuck up and take action. Whether you feel like it or not.

Relying on motivation is like handing over your power to something external. Real fire comes from within. The world is yours! It's about decisions. Decide to be the driver of your destiny, not a passenger waiting for the next wave of motivation to carry you forward.

A great coach won't motivate you. That's not their job. Their job is to hold up a mirror and force you to face the habits, fears, and excuses holding you back. They'll guide you to uncover your own strength. A coach helps you say, "I AM," not "I will," and

"IT'S DONE," not "I'm trying". Motivation whispers, but power roars.

Motivation isn't some magical force that comes before action—it's the other way around.

Action motivates motivation.

You don't feel like hitting the gym until you're there and you start sweating. You don't feel like studying until you open your book and start reading. You don't feel like making the effort to get to know new people until you're out and mingling.

Act first; motivation will follow.

Amor Fati

Your worldview isn't just in your head, it's also shaped by what you do out there. Forget convincing yourself that you're something! Let your actions define you.

Don't wait to feel like the person you want to be. Act like it, and the feelings will catch up.

Experience is the real teacher. Fumbling is part of the learning curve.

If you want to make something, make it. Scarcity isn't in resources; it's in initiative.

A perfect future doesn't need a crystal ball. It needs a string of right actions.

There's no formula for greatness. Lean into what works, even if it's against the norm. Action is wild, it's messy, it's creation in all its chaos.

Comfort is death. It causes depression and anxiety. Action throws you into discomfort, makes you hustle in the unknown.

That consistent grind? It sets you on a path where time works for you, where life develops for you.

Action isn't just revealing paths; it is the path. It's faith in the present, giving you eyes beyond standing still. It harmonizes your internal and external worlds, making sense of the chaos.

A map is handy, but you have to walk the streets. Action is change, and staying still isn't a goal—it's a trap.

Fail in action? That's not failure—it's a process, a journey. The failure of inaction? That's the real killer, eating away at your soul.

Action is revolutionary. Real change comes from the silent ones getting stuff done.

You might not get why you're doing something right away, but have faith. Action takes time to unfold, and the lessons learned in the process run deep.

You've already decided before you're conscious of it. Action doesn't justify itself—it adjusts based on what's happening, not on some made-up stories. So shut up and act. Adjust yourself on the move, and let your actions define your story.

***

Action isn't just about doing, it's also about not doing when it's the right move.

Waiting can be the toughest action. It's not laziness, it's disciplined self-control. Patience, like a sniper's precision, is a powerful action.

Relaxation, when done right, is an action—a recharge after vigorous action. Don't let it turn into laziness! It's about maintaining balance.

Imagination is action in the mind. It's not about escaping reality but deepening your connection to it. Visualization is a mental action, creating neural connections that impact your physical actions.

Observation is another form of action. Learn from others. Go to the source, watch, and emulate.

Epiphanies—we all have them, but the real power lies in the actions that follow. Don't dwell on being unique when having the epiphany! Be unique in the actions you take afterward. That's where your power and uniqueness truly shine.

***

Our habits wield immense power, shaping the contours of our existence. From the way we eat to the patterns of our thoughts and work, habits are the architects of our daily default. Tapping into this reality, we discover that molding these default actions is akin to unlocking a cascade of impact. The initial struggle of adopting positive habits evolves into a seamless routine, proving that persistence is the alchemy of transformation.

Environments, too, hold sway over your well-being. Simple actions, like forging new friendships or cleaning your space becomes a weekly sanity pact, a small action with daily benefits.

What gets measured gets managed!

Is the glass half-full or half-empty? Who gives a fuck! It's the one who grabs the glass, drinks, and refills it that is in control.

Stagnation creeps in when we convince ourselves of needing complete knowledge. But action, accepting the potential of failure, becomes the gateway to transcending our ignorance.

Time favors the dynamic over the stagnant. Time crafts opportunities and breathes life into potentialities through action.

Stagnation yields to the forward momentum of those who dare to act. Like sharks that must swim to breathe, action becomes the oxygen that sustains life.

Action is the force that kills the illusion of fear and harnesses time's power towards monumental achievements. It is the defiant antidote to stagnation, the force that transforms the ordinary into the extraordinary.

When doubt creeps in, seek alternative perspectives, or quit. But take action!

Valor is found in actions, not outcomes. The unpredictable nature of life, rife with randomness, underscores the futility of letting results dictate your path. Focus on the nobility of your actions, for in the chaos, actions define character.

Actions, not words, shape rituals, anchoring us in a mental space where consistency breeds clarity and purpose.

The path forward demands a willingness to evolve, embracing change based on newfound insights. Ditch the fear of contradicting yourself. Deciding is progress. Embrace the power of good choices and value progress over the illusion of perfection.

Nobody is successful without being unsuccessful. Nobody is perfect. There is a raw humanity beneath triumph. Victory is forged not in perfection but in relentless action, unwavering focus, and the occasional stroke of luck.

STOP trying to be perfect!

***

Embrace the game! Happiness is not found in its attainment, but in its pursuit.

Happiness is designed to keep us running. Nature doesn't care if you're happy. Its game is survival and procreation, and happiness is simply bait on the hook. Our ancestors didn't have it easy. They weren't lounging around waiting to feel motivated. They fought, hunted, built, and strived, always chasing more. The discontented ones, the relentless ones, outbred and outlived the losers who dared to sit still and smile.

In truth, happiness as a permanent state is dangerous. Contentment breeds complacency, and complacency gets you killed. The ones who survived weren't happy; they were hungry. And so, we inherited this endless hunger—the inability to ever have enough, be enough, or achieve enough. Insatiability is our legacy.

Happiness isn't a destination; it's a high. It comes and goes. We're built to chase it, not hold it. Strong relationships, good health, purpose, generosity, and a mindset of gratitude—you can't passively wait for these things. You have to fight for them.

True happiness isn't about eliminating struggle. It's about choosing your struggles. It's about being grateful for what you have without comparison. It's about mastering your emotions, accepting yourself, and understanding that happiness will come and go.

***

Remember what I said about explaining yourself? It's endless and draining and self-defeating. Shift from 'why' to 'why not'.

Preserve your energy for tackling real issues instead of meandering through imagined problems.

Luxury breeds inaction. Those born into ease lack the impetus for action, contrasting sharply with those forged in adversity. Action becomes a response to necessity, a testament to resilience.

Keep moving forward! Inaction is death.

Persistence is an unstoppable force against setbacks.

"It ain't about how hard you hit... It's about how hard you can get hit and keep moving forward."

In the game of life, persistence is victory.

Some goals may be unattainable. Yet the pursuit retains its worth.

***

There are no shortcuts to inspiration. Those who aspire to greatness must traverse the path of intense and prolonged practice. The tales of instant success fail to illuminate the backdrop of commitment, endurance, and personal tribulations. Inspiration reveals itself to those who toil diligently, forging a symbiotic relationship with action.

Action is the relentless force that transforms inspiration from an ephemeral spark into a sustained flame, illuminating the path toward mastery.

Action implies risk-taking and the willingness to be wrong. It involves investing something of value, differentiating yourself from passive onlookers.

Courage... it's not something you already have that makes you brave when times get tough. You earn it when you've survived the storm; not by chance, but by guts and glory. If you do not have courage to take a risk, you will never amount to anything.

Immerse yourself so profoundly in whatever you do that there's no space for fear. After enduring setbacks, failures, and tears, you'll gaze upon the messy progress made, the unpredictable path navigated, and the brave heart earned. In that moment, the initial fear will be forgotten, replaced by a sense of accomplishment born from relentless action.

***

Action isn't just a sequence of movements; it brings new possibilities. Every step taken in a particular direction spawns opportunities, causing alternative paths to diminish. You wield the power to choose the direction in which your potential futures materialize, engaging with the force of emergence daily—whether for good or ill.

The commitment to action unleashes a magical force; it attracts unforeseen events, encounters, and support. The decision to act triggers a stream of incidents that align with your commitment.

Action serves as the equilibrium between past, present, and future. When thoughts become entangled in the past or future, the present gets overshadowed. Balancing action restores harmony among temporal dimensions.

Creativity burgeonsthrivesflourishes when the mind shifts from consumption to creation through action. Engaging in a task propels the mind into a creative mode, fostering improvement and production.

Action sharpens intuition. True intuition development arises from taking action. Decision-making abilities, especially under time constraints, flourish through consistent practice.

The flow state is attainable through focused, deliberate practice—action.

In this abundance of content, action becomes a filter for consumption. Amid the deluge of attention-seeking headlines and demands for our time, focusing on action clarifies what's worth reading, watching, or learning. It serves as a guide, steering attention to content with genuine value.

***

Do you think you can predict the future? Your false sense of confidence blinds you to the unpredictability of life. Action serves as a vital antidote, grounding you in the present and fostering resilience to face the unknown.

Action encourages serendipity, allowing for unexpected discoveries along the journey. The open and aware, not the stagnant or narrow-minded, embrace the beauty of chance encounters and opportunities that arise while moving forward.

Action's beauty lies in the messy aftermath—the zig-zagging path, scarred face, broken heart—reflecting true confidence born of experience. Unlike the superficial façade of beauty, action's beauty deepens with time, embracing the imperfections that define the journey.

While imagination can propel us forward, action reminds us of the battles of the flesh intertwined with the mind. Knowledge without practice breeds dangerous arrogance, and success without the struggle of action leaves one vulnerable. Action teaches that nobody is invincible, grounding us in reality.

Action is the ultimate test, determining possibilities through effort and audacity rather than relying on speculative predictions. It's not about knowing what will work; it's about finding out through the courageous pursuit of action.

Treating life as an experiment allows us to swiftly and inexpensively run tests, urging us to focus on solutions rather than fixating on causes.

Error, when met with right action, transforms into valuable information. Recognize the significance of your failures, learn from them, and progress. Action unveils our true capabilities, dispelling the distorted perceptions generated by the ego.

Action is positioned as a sense-maker in the face of chaos, providing clarity where abstraction leads to frustration. It dismantles the notion that understanding must precede action, arguing that full comprehension often follows engagement.

Action builds momentum, fostering a positive cycle of behaviour. Consistency prevails against daily obstacles, ensuring progress. Regret, often stemming from acts of omission, fades when met with action. Chronic regrets persist when one fails to act, while engaging in action offers immediate relief.

Turn your weaknesses into strengths through action. Leverage your weaknesses as a launching pad for transformative action, personal growth, and achievement.

The challenges you face and the difficult tasks you undertake contribute to your personal growth. Superheroes require supervillains to showcase their capabilities. The underdog often triumphs because they confront greater forces, drawing on energy and strength that the comfortable lack. Some goals might seem impossible, but action is the process of making the impossible possible.

Action serves as a humbling force, forcing you to confront overlooked details and unforeseen challenges. It is an equalizer that brings you back to reality.

Questions that often lead to overthinking, such as "Why am I doing this?" or "What is my purpose?" are better addressed through action, not endless justification.

Action reframes your mindset, shifting focus from doubts to opportunities and allowing you to build a culture of your own creation.

Repetitive action sharpens skills, making it easier to bounce back after setbacks. It builds tolerance for failures, transforming it into a tool for learning and correction. Action seizes opportunities, especially in moments of chaos.

Action kills stress—you're too busy to overthink. It trains you for composure under pressure, keeping you cool-headed through exposure and preparation. And wasting time? That's impossible—every action fuels progress and deepens awareness.

Taking action illuminates the true dream, helping you differentiate between desires and passions. It defies constant questioning and comparison. The only real story is in your actions.

***

Focus on something real. Don't get caught up in society's expectations and cultural distractions.

Flip the script!

School is cool and ain't nothing wrong with a job—as long as you're valued and respected. But don't go chase a degree, a job, and a bunch of shit you don't really need just because it's what you think "they" want from you. Do what you want of you!

Prioritize authentic connections, emotional highs, genuine relationships, and personal ambitions over conformity to standards. Your value is not defined by the number of degrees or material possessions you have.

Reclaim your mind!

Take control of your thoughts and actions. Resist the external pressures that aim to shape you into a conformist consumer.

Live your life intentionally, free from the influence of cultural engineers trying to mold you into a passive consumer of manufactured, meaningless content.

Rebel against the expectations of society. Pursue a more genuine, fulfilling existence.

Take control of your own cultural experience instead of passively consuming media.

Create your own cultural narrative. Challenge the influence of MSM, Hollywood, and manipulated history narratives—shape your own beliefs, values, and lifestyle, rather than allowing external media to dictate these aspects.

Break free from the influence of mass-produced, superficial content.

Live your life as a unique journey. Authentic and self-reliant.

Don't idolize celebrities and try to be like them. It takes away your power by shifting your attention from your own life to shallow goals set by the media. Most of them are full of shit, anyway... Be yourself—everyone else is taken.

Reclaim your autonomy, think independently, and actively shape your own cultural experience.

It's the work that counts, every single time. The work to love, create, and live.

Shape your world to force the right actions. What can you do today that your future self will thank you for?

In life, the step in front of you is the most important thing. The biggest opportunity is always right now.

Simplify the process with action. Action simplifies while dealing with complex problems, allowing for improvisation.

Continuous right action is tough. Surprises make us flinch, but use that flinch as a trigger. Lean into it. Don't fear it.

Stop considering whether you should, and stop considering if you're ready.

Procrastination is a fancy excuse for losers who just don't have balls.

Action pushes you higher. Problems don't get smaller; they get bigger. But you get stronger.

Leave the world with a reminder that you were here. Spread whatever you are. The way you are in life matters more than what you get in life.

The choice is yours, and yours alone. Everything you do matters.

Decide. Commit. Conquer.

Rituals

What's the difference between winners and losers? Are they born with it—lucky, or gifted? Absolutely not. It's not luck, it's discipline. It's in their habits. Not just routines thrown together to get by, but intentional, sharpened rituals that define who they are. While most people let habits control them, winners are architects, designing their daily actions like a blueprint for greatness.

For the last decade, I've been the mad scientist of my own habits, diving deep into the mechanics of motivation, psychology, and self-mastery. It's been an obsession, a relentless quest to uncover what drives transformation. But change—it's terrifying, a leap into the unknown. Staring down the vast abyss of possibility can freeze even the boldest soul. That's where strategy comes in. Forget leaping blind into the fire. We lean in—gently, but persistently—until fear shrinks to nothing more than a whisper.

Here's the trick: start small, almost absurdly small. Make the habit so manageable, so effortless, that your mind can't fight back.

Reading a book a week sounds impossible? Start with one a month. Fifty push-ups every day feels brutal? Start with five. Cold plunge is too intimidating? Try a cold shower. Inch by inch, you rewire yourself, turning these tiny wins into undeniable proof of progress. Soon, these habits won't be things you have to do—they'll be things you can't imagine living without. In the beginning, forget massive leaps. The real secret? Consistency. Show up, every single day, and watch the small victories transform into unstoppable momentum.

Always do the thing at least a tiny bit, even if not as much as you planned. Sometimes, all you need is a few minutes to get in the zone. So… JUST DO IT!

Minuscule alterations act as catalysts for metamorphic results. Baby steps!

***

Triggers are the hidden forces shaping your habits. Understand them, and you unlock control over your daily actions.

Triggers can be anything—a place, a time, a feeling, the people you're with, or even what you just did. Once you see the cycle for what it is, you've taken the first step to breaking free and building habits on your own terms.

The easiest way to build a new habit? Attach it to something you already do. Don't force it—let it flow. Ask yourself, *"What does this naturally follow?"* Find the rhythm in your routine. *After I do (a), I'll move right into (b).* Like making your bed after you wake up—no debate, no resistance. Think mornings: quiet, automatic, one step leading to the next. That's the secret. Not willpower. Not motivation. Just momentum. By letting one small step follow the next, seamlessly, like links in a chain.

Face it, failure is inevitable. But failure doesn't mean you're a failure—it means you didn't plan for the storm. When it rains, it pours. Visualizing success is all well and good, but we often forget the setbacks. Anticipate the storm. Plan for the rain and specify how you'll stay dry. You can't prepare for everything, but priming for likely setbacks shields you against willpower meltdowns.

Everywhere you look, there are temptations conditioning you for pleasure. Predictable feedback loops don't cut it. Experiences with finite variability become less engaging because they eventually become predictable. To counteract the monotony and keep interest alive, you must introduce variable rewards. Habits with unpredictable rewards are the ones that hook us for life. Make it so the completion of your new habit comes to be associated with the reward you enjoy after. When a behaviour becomes neurologically associated with a reward, the craving for that reward merges with a new craving for the behaviour itself.

Stop rewarding yourself for no fucking reason!

Our environment shapes us. If you keep unhealthy foods at home, that's all you'll eat. Redesign your realm! Make the wanted habits accessible and the unwanted ones elusive. Want to stop getting stoned? Stop hanging out with your stoner friends. Want to stop wasting time on social media? Delete the apps, or at least remove them from your home screen. You can also turn your phone display to greyscale, which will make looking at pictures and videos less appealing. Want to play fewer video games? Unplug your console and put it away. Want to hit the gym in the morning? Get your bag ready and go to sleep early. Remember, make the habit simple to do, and it'll take care of itself.

Life is full of scorecards. But beware, these scorecards can distort priorities, pulling us toward short-term outcomes and away from the learning process. Learning habits is an art, a skill like any other. Count the right things. Set a number, log your activity, and record what you did well, where you fucked up, and what you can improve daily. Celebrate those daily wins, identify unforeseen obstacles, and focus on the daily victories. Momentum is a force to be reckoned with.

Ever notice how productivity shoots up when someone's watching? The imagined social consequences keep us on the straight and narrow line. Accountability is no joke. And if you're serious about behaviour change, throw in some stakes. A goal without consequences is just wishful thinking. The right incentives? Accountability and stakes. They keep us on the path when the going gets tough. Turn it into a game—a thirty-day challenge with a donation to an "anti-charity" on the line. That's a commitment!

How long does it take to form a habit? Forget the one-size-fits-all myth. Science says between 18 and 254 days, but around 66 days is the average. Individuality is key; habits ingrained for years will need varied timelines for transformation.

Habits are individual and resistant to universal formulas.

Identify habits worth nurturing. A peek into the routines of high achievers provides cues, but your priorities, visions, and goals determine the ideal habits.

What should you stop or start?

Don't try to change your whole life overnight; you'll drown in the complexity. Pick one habit, let it root, then introduce another. Success doesn't come overnight!

***

Your most important goal must be handled first.

Your willpower is a finite source. It depletes as the day progresses. The more you wrestle with temptation, the more you push yourself to do the hard thing, the less willpower you'll have left in your tank. Anything that requires some sort of effort depletes your willpower.

In the morning, or whenever you get your ass up out of bed, your battery is charged-up. That's why doing the hard thing first in the morning is always easier.

Rituals

Whatever you have to do, whatever you want to do, do it first thing in the morning.

If you can't muster up the strength or motivation to kickstart, it's likely that your willpower is on life support, or maybe, just maybe, it ain't that important to you...

Decode your own motivational cycles, seeing when you naturally feel up or down, then you'll have a better idea about where to place your new habits.

***

Every thought, action, and emotion—like an architect's blueprint—constructs the foundation of your reality.

Your journey starts with awareness, illuminating the shadows of your existence.

Mindfulness is the gateway to recognizing negative patterns and replacing them with positive ones.

Your ego is your biggest enemy. It's a real battle, an internal struggle. I've faced this challenge, confronted by the resistance to metamorphosis. My desires—strong and resolute—overcame the fear, leading to the unfolding of my life's design.

From financial freedom to professional success, from optimal health to spiritual awakenings, it all comes down to choices. The genesis is the mind—the loom where thoughts turn into beliefs.

Why, then, do you abstain from the daily alchemy of mental and physical exertion? The answer lies in belief—or, more precisely, the lack thereof. If belief were a driving force, why are goals not respected, diets neglected, and dreams un-chased?

Why?

I've been there, masterfully crafting excuses to play a lesser role in life, hooked to the addiction of emotional dependency. Remember, every thought triggers a cascade of hormonal, chemical, and physical changes. Altering this equilibrium is a perceived stress, an adversary to change.

***

Habit is the driving force of your life; what you do every day determines who you are. Study the people you admire and mirror their habits. Build the habits that will help you become the person you wish to be.

The ten thousand hour rule isn't just a theory—it's a fact of life. The more you do it, the more it sticks.

Focus on who you want to be tomorrow, not who you were yesterday.

Stop looking for *Angels*, start looking for *Angles*.

HABIT is the strongest Force of life
WILLPOWER is the ENERGY you use to get into habit
SELF-DISCIPLINE is what you practice to build up
WILLPOWER
Practice SELF-DISCIPLINE by exercising SELF-CONTROL

Linguistic Magic

Words are sorcery. They alter the fabric of perception and even reality.

Words, not by nature supernatural, possess a magical essence. How we speak, both to ourselves and others, carries the potential for destructive curses or captivating enchantments, much like magic. Words serve as conduits to our thoughts, carrying the vibrational energy of intentions.

In the realm of psychology, focused on social dynamics and communication, complex language emerges as a distinctly human tool for conveying intricate ideas. The true magic of words unfolds in interpersonal exchanges, where language crafts vivid mental images, transferring concepts through careful descriptions. Through this linguistic sorcery, one can create illusions or hallucinations, altering perceptions with the simple power of words.

Though words can vividly describe objects, the most potent use of words lies in shaping ideas and beliefs. Effectively communicating a set of beliefs can fundamentally alter another's worldview. In this way, words bear the potential for life-altering transformations, introducing ideas so profound that they reshape one's perception of reality.

Thoughts breed words that manifest into experiences. The quality of our thoughts and words determines the essence of our reality. High-vibration expressions give birth to a life of dreams, while low-vibration impure expressions manifest a nightmare reality.

Elevating our vibration involves adopting a high-vibration vocabulary. Our words are energetic forces that influence our energy levels. To understand this, breathe deep, absorb the energy of words like "sad" and "happy", and observe the shifts within.

Words hold the power to bless or curse. They echo the beliefs cast upon us, forming 'I am' statements that sculpt our reality. Words can break or liberate.

Quantum physics supports the idea that consciousness might be an architect of reality. The theory suggests that the observer's thoughts and intentions could influence quantum-level events, reflecting on the profound link between reality and consciousness pondered by philosophers.

Dr. Masaru Emoto, an innovative Japanese scientist, studied how thoughts and intentions shape the physical realm. For over two decades until his passing in 2014, Dr. Emoto analyzed how the molecular structure of water undergoes a metamorphosis when exposed to human words, thoughts, sounds, and intentions.

His revolutionary research revealed that water forms beautiful molecular structures when influenced by positive human intentions, while negative intentions result in distorted, unattractive formations. These findings were uncovered using Magnetic Resonance Analysis technology and high-speed photography.

His studies demonstrated that polluted and toxic water, when subjected to prayer and positive intention, can undergo a transformation, restoring it to beautifully formed geometric crystals, like those found in clean, healthy water.

Emoto's research expanded to explore how sound impacts water. Classical music generated beautiful crystalline patterns, while heavy metal music produced distorted formations.

Linguistic Magic

Dr. Masaru Emoto discovered water as a living consciousness. He illuminated the invisible energy within water, revealing the profound impact that human thoughts, sounds, and intentions wield.

If water is influenced by words, intentions, and energies, what about human beings, composed mostly of water? The transformative power of thoughts on the water we're made of opens a realm of possibilities.

What makes words so potent? Why do they wield the kind of power that defines our capabilities and potential? And how can we harness this linguistic magic for our own advantage?

Language in all its forms—signs, symbols, written word, spoken word—is pure magic. It's how we share ideas, communicate, and spark change in ourselves and others.

The choices we make with our language set the parameters of our lives. The way we express ourselves can either be the key to unlocking personal and professional success or the trapdoor to failure, pain, and death. The magic with words is about the meanings we give 'em and how we interpret life, not just about their dictionary definitions

Deciphering the meaning of the events that unfold in your life and deciding to find an empowering meaning is a power move. You mess with the meaning, and suddenly, you're either on the victory lap or stuck in despair.

Take failing a test, getting fired from a job, or getting dumped by your partner... Does that mean you're a certified failure? Or does it mean you've just found out what you need to improve? It's all up to you to decide. Even if failure slaps you in the face, you can step in and flip the script. Transform that failure into a stepping stone for improvement. Reframe that shit!

The power of words isn't just about the words themselves. It's about the emotions they bring. Your internal dialogue, the shit you tell yourself—that's where the struggle is. If you're constantly feeding your brain self-deprecating crap like you're fat, broke, weak, worthless, or stupid, you're letting words strip you of the power to see the silver lining in your experiences. You're letting them affirm your worst beliefs about yourself.

Emotions, events, human connections—they're all puppets dangling from the strings of linguistics. If you want to be the puppet master, start by understanding the raw power in what you say, whether it's to yourself or the people around you.

Words aren't just sounds, symbols, or thoughts; they're spells, and the way you use them matters. Say "I hate you" with a smirk and a chuckle, and you'll get a different reaction than if you bellow it with rage.

Words are like renegades, infiltrating the minds of those who receive them. Depending on their mental state, they might interpret your words in ways you never intended, especially with text messages. We've all been there, decoding a text message like it's the Rosetta Stone, searching for emotional clues or hidden meanings.

Don't go searching for meaning without considering the tone, facial expressions, and body language; and when reading a text message, be careful to not take things simply at their face value, keep an open heart, and don't take things too personal. Words have a life of their own, both in their delivery and their reception.

Now, pay attention—the power of words doesn't just lie in their vocalization; it's also in how you let 'em seep into your soul.

Linguistic Magic

Whether you're talking, writing, or just thinking, words are forces of nature, shaping your trajectory to greatness or leaving you lost in disillusionment.

You're sculpting your expressions based on a blend of your upbringing, your environment, and the media you've consumed. Most of us are like kids playing with dynamite, not realizing the explosive power behind our words. We let the words of others bomb us, showering us with emotional chaos.

We're victims of words, passive participants in the game of life without understanding the rules of language.

Become an architect of words. Build that verbal expression arsenal, choose your words wisely, and put some emotional force behind them. Be vigilant about how others' words affect you. Misinterpretations can be a bitch, and sometimes, we tolerate words that we shouldn't.

Don't ignore the power of words; it's a force that'll keep playing in the background of your life. Your ability to find love and joy? It hinges on the frequency of those words, whether they're sought, expressed, received, or understood.

***

The word "spell" is a descendant of the ninth-century word 'spel', which meant incantation, charm, influence, magical powers, and fascination.

Now, after reviewing Dr. Masaru Emoto's research, I'm guessing you understand the weight your words carry. When you hear certain words, whether from others or in your own head, you know the kind of impact they can have on your thoughts.

A word means nothing until we attach a meaning to it or someone teaches it to us. It's all about our own perception, deciding if a word is good, bad, loving, hateful, positive, negative, or whatever.

With over seven billion people on this planet, that's seven billion-plus meanings and perceptions floating around. And let me tell you, a lot are getting offended over stuff that's basically made up.

Your words, or let's call them spells, are powerful. Watch them, listen to them—those words create mental images, meanings, and feelings. They shape your reality. With fifty thousand thoughts a day, you're basically playing make-believe.

"It's easier to destroy than create." Spells have the power to inspire love or instill fear.

Sometimes we've got these enchantments in our heads, like 'The world is a cruel place', 'Money is evil', 'Successful people are different from me', 'Things are never going to change for me', 'I'm not good enough', 'Who do I think I am?', or the classic 'My life has no meaning'. That's some serious influence and power!

'I am' are the two most powerful words in the world. What follows those words shapes the world you see, live in, and ultimately experience.

Becoming impeccable with your word demands honesty and truthfulness, building trust and self-worth. This applies both outwardly and inwardly, so watch your self-talk.

An exercise for self-reflection—face a mirror and carefully listen to the words you use to describe yourself. Replace non-serving 'I am' statements, transform existing words, and craft affirmations. This simple yet profound practice serves as a crucial step toward positive transformation.

In essence, our words, born from thoughts, shape our reality. By understanding this dynamic, you can consciously harness the power of words, casting spells that illuminate your path to a fulfilling life.

Be impeccable with your words!

BODY

Health Is Wealth

Money comes, money goes. You can always get you some more—and by all means, please do. But health is wealth!

You can't buy it back once it's gone. It's worth more than a Rolex, more than a Lamborghini, more than a mansion in Palm Beach. It's priceless!

No amount of money can replace the joy of a pain-free existence and a mind at peace.

Money is important. But without good health, you can't enjoy it. What good is all the money in the world when your knees buckle, when your heart is in trouble, or your brain struggles? You can't cash in on your financial success if you're hooked to a hospital monitor or dead.

A peaceful mind and a body that can still run, lift, breathe deep, and wake up ready to fight another day? That's a real privilege. Chase that. Because no stack of cash can match the freedom of a body and mind in harmony.

Health is wealth and wealth is health. You make more money by being more healthy. You have that edge! Your hands are steady and your mind is sharp. Flip the coin, though, and watch how quickly the game changes. When health crashes, your finances are the first casualty.

Being sick is expensive. From a broken leg to depression, everything has a price tag. Sickness robs your future. In the real world, vitality wins. Every single time.

Live longer, earn longer—simple math. A healthy body gives you more years to hustle, more time to compound investments, more opportunities to stack wins and grow your empire. It's not just about surviving—it's about thriving.

It's hard to enjoy your bread when you're dead. Health breeds wealth.

Without health, you're not living—you're just existing. A fat bank account won't mean a thing when your body's crumbling, your energy is drained, and joy feels like a distant memory. What's the point of winning the race if you're too broken to celebrate at the finish line?

Prioritize your health and the wealth will chase you.

Real wealth is a life so rich in strength, purpose, and fire that every dollar you earn feels like a bonus.

You Are What You Eat

The body becomes what the foods are; as the spirit becomes what the thoughts are.

They say you are what you eat. Food is energy. Energy is the currency of the universe.

Animals and plants have memory. They feel. They might not express emotions like we do, but they resonate with the vibrations of life and death, love, and terror, the same way we do. When you put something inside your body, you are taking in that memory, that frequency, that emotion. Think of it as an exchange of raw energy, a trade of memories encoded in the flesh.

***

Walk into any average grocery store, and the meat you see is harvested from a factory of suffering. Let's call it what it is—prison-farmed animals, raised in the brutal conditions of industrialized agriculture. These animals don't know freedom; they know confinement, anxiety, stress, and misery. Every muscle fiber, every sinew, hums with the trauma of that existence, and when you take it in, you inherit that residue of torment.

There's science to it, too. A stressed animal, slaughtered within hours of psychological or physical agony, delivers meat that is darker, drier, off—and you can taste it. Compare that to wild game, and the difference is staggering. Wild animals roam free, unshackled, carrying the taste of a life lived on their terms, fed by nature, not force.

Fruits and vegetables are no different!

Growing evidence, from various scientific studies, points to a concerning decline in essential nutrients within our crops. Most fruits, vegetables, and grains are now depleted in protein, calcium, phosphorus, iron, riboflavin, and vitamin C. Industrial farming has squeezed the soil dry, robbing the Earth of the minerals that once fueled our strength. We're consuming empty food.

Yes…What the Fuck!

Modern agriculture puts profits over quality—an endless push for higher yields, faster growth, and aesthetic perfection. The land that once held life-giving minerals and vitamins is now overworked, exhausted, forced to produce more at the expense of quality. These quick-fix practices—irrigation overloads, synthetic fertilizers, and the constant cycle of disruptive harvesting—leave soil stripped of its vitality, unable to nourish plants with the minerals we desperately need.

The very life force within our food is sacrificed for crops that ship well and look good, as if that's what fuels the human body. Crops are bred for higher yields and visual appeal, with minimal emphasis on vital vitamin and mineral content. The value of food is in the nutrients, not the appearance—but that's not what makes money!

Many studies highlight the extent of nutrient decline, indicating substantial reductions in protein, iron, zinc, and various vitamins in crops. Grains experienced a 23% decrease in protein content from 1955 to 2016, and potatoes a 100% loss of vitamin A, 57% of vitamin C and iron, and 28% of calcium. And even meat suffers, as livestock feed on grasses and grains sapped of their own nutrition. [55, 56]

The quest for volume (PROFITS) has robbed our food of its essence.

***

Organic is the only way to go!

Organic embraces the entire process of growing and processing agricultural products, including fruits, vegetables, grains, dairy, and meat. The focus is on improving soil and water quality, reducing pollution, ensuring humane living conditions for farm animals, and establishing a self-sustaining resource cycle on the farm. The use of artificial fertilizers, sewage sludge, synthetic pesticides, radiation, and genetic engineering are restricted. Organic farmers rely on plant waste, green manure, compost, and natural pesticides to build a self-sustaining ecosystem.

The standards are strict, and only certified products wear the official Organic seal. But don't let labels like "free range" and "humane" fool you—they're marketing ploys designed to sell the same brutal practices with a more palatable name. Be cautious and read the labels, because a lot of companies try to swindle you.

"Organic" and "natural" are not the same. When you see "natural" slapped on a label, it simply means there are no artificial colors or preservatives, but it says nothing about farming practices. Don't fall for the illusion of purity.

***

Just as organic farming restores the life force to your food, clean water is essential to keep your body pure—because what you drink is as critical as what you eat.

Water is essential, but the wrong source could poison you!

In urban areas, tap water is often laced with chemicals and contaminants—arsenic, chlorine, fluoride, pesticides like atrazine—that are dangerous to your health and overall well-being. [46]

You don't need a chemistry degree to know this stuff's toxic.

If you're stuck with city tap water, filter it. Better yet, go for spring water.

Health Consciousness

Diets help you reshape habits, amplify health consciousness, and embrace an active lifestyle.

This is where choices have to align with who you are at the core. Sustainability matters, and the diet that sticks is the one that works with your lifestyle, not against it.

No single diet works for everyone. Whatever you do, stay away from processed sugars. Sugar feeds cancer. [57]

You're playing a dangerous game if you don't take your diet seriously. Poor nutrition opens the door to diabetes, heart disease, and cancer. Your diet is your weapon against these afflictions. Life isn't about compromise but about commanding the best possible version of yourself.

When you prioritize health, you're building a fortress around your body—a defence that keeps illness away while setting you up for a vibrant life. Every thoughtful choice, every gradual shift towards balanced nutrition, isn't just a diet; it's an evolution. It's the road where the rewards of healthy eating reveal themselves slowly, with each step adding strength, vitality, and resilience to your life.

A real diet isn't just about nutrition; it's fuel for a state of constant vitality. Wellness shouldn't just be an aim but a lifestyle. You commit not only to fuel but to thrive, letting every choice add to the quality of your existence, bringing energy, clarity, and purpose to every waking moment.

You Are What You Eat

***

Some foods just don't play well together. You'd think it's no big deal, but there's a reason why you feel sluggish after you eat a burger and fries. I know, you really can't have one without the other. But the truth is that meat and carbs just don't mix well in your stomach.

Your body needs an alkaline base to digest starches but an acidic base for digesting proteins. Here's a chemistry lesson: opposites (acid and alkali) can't coexist—they cancel each other out. Throw protein and carbs together in your stomach, and digestion becomes a mess. Undigested food becomes a breeding ground for bacteria, triggering fermentation and digestive problems.

Mix the wrong foods, and you'll lose your energy—that's how you get sick. Excess acid thickens the blood, slowing its flow, robbing your body of the lifeblood—oxygen. Have you ever felt the *itis* (food coma)? It's not because you ate too much food—although it doesn't help. It's because you mixed too many different foods together.

Do yourself a favor and stick to one concentrated food at a meal. What's concentrated? Anything not packed with water.

Digestion should be easy, not exhausting. Food is fuel, not a dead weight.

If you want to live a longer and healthier life, you need to be conscious of what you eat, how you eat it, and what you eat it with.

God Body

Without strength, we are weak. Weak men are easy to kill. Power comes to those who push their bodies to the limits.

Testosterone is the essence of what makes men, men. Forget about sex and libido—it's about vitality, energy, and drive.

The truth is that your grandfather probably had higher testosterone than you do, thanks to cleaner diets, more active lifestyles, and less chemical interference from modern food and water.

Beyond clean eating and pumping iron, testosterone feels like the one thing you can't cheat—a genetic lottery ticket you either won or didn't. But that's a lie sold to the weak. Testosterone is like fire; you don't wait for it, you ignite it. Take action, push limits, and watch the cycle feed itself. You grind, you conquer, and in return, your body rewards you with the primal fuel of progress. Get shit done, and you won't just feel more powerful—you'll become it.

You want to feel like Superman? Optimize your testosterone! High testosterone levels increase your mental and physical energy, sharpen your competitive edge, and even help prevent neurodegenerative diseases. You want more muscle? More strength? A body that feels invincible? There's no big secret! Go to war and conquer!

Every set you push through, every morning you show up when you don't feel like it, every plateau you smash builds unshakable willpower.

Power is for the disciplined, the relentless, the unforgiving. A strong body is a gateway. To energy. To focus. To success.

***

As I stood there, staring at my reflection after months of hard work, I expected to see a chiseled demigod staring back at me. But reality was much more subtle.

In everything you do, day-to-day gains are sneaky and subtle. If you don't track those changes yourself, months of grinding can feel like nothing. That's how motivation dies. And when it does, quitting seems justified. That's why you've always got to remember where you started.

Now let's get one thing straight, the gym ain't a social club, it's a battleground. And you? You're the lone warrior. Lock in. This is your moment. You're not here to impress. You're here to conquer.

Goals are important. "Getting in shape"? That's vague. Be real, be specific. Short-term goals are easier to achieve, and they build on top of each other. Don't expect to become Schwarzenegger overnight. Rome wasn't built in a day, and neither is a six-pack. Start at the roots and celebrate your ascent from the bottom.

It's about tapping into your potential and turning those dormant abilities into a success story. Look at your life and kill the habits dragging you back.

Comfort zones? Fuck that! No pain, no gain. If you're expecting life to be easy, do yourself a favor—forget about your dreams. You're not built for this.

Stop waiting for the stars to align or for motivation to be strong. It's not about showing up when your schedule is clear and you pumped up. What matters is getting your ass up when you don't feel like it. That's how winners are made.

Consistency is key! Life throws hard moments at you to test you.

Pick the path that paves the way to your goals, not the one with the tempting shortcuts. Future you will thank you.

Now you're committed. Get your mind in the game. No more fucking around. Less planning, more doing.

***

End each set in failure. There's no pride in half-passing anything.

Weight choice? That's on you! Just don't try to prove anything. Start small and build up little by little.

Low reps with heavy weight tends to increase muscle mass, while high reps with light weight increases muscle endurance.

Symmetry is beauty. Keep it even!

Safety ain't a joke.

Safety ain't a joke. Injuries are setbacks.

Safety ain't a joke. Injuries are setbacks. Minimize risk.

Do I make myself clear? Stretch. Warm up. Get your fucking form on point! Don't add weight on the bar if you're not ready for it. Quality over quantity—every time. Keep your core strong. Cool down properly.

Breakdown, then repair.

Eat right. Eat more if you want some size, but don't go full Arnold with it. You want something sustainable—something you can manage with consistency. So take it easy and build smart.

***

How much time do you really want to sacrifice to exercise? Because if being super swole isn't your top priority, then you might want to forget about trying to hit every single muscle independently. When you're just starting out, trying to maximize time and actually make progress, it's the compound movements like squats, deadlifts, push-ups and pull-ups that matter most. These multi-joint exercises hit multiple muscle groups all at once.

Muscle isolation workout plans are built for a life that revolves around the gym, demanding you to show up five or six days a week, no excuses. One day you're pushing chest, the next you're pulling back, then it's leg day, arms and shoulders, and a day for cardio. Rest, repeat. It works—if you have that kind of time and commitment. But miss a day, and the whole system falls apart.

Time is a rare currency. A routine that fits your life and can be done consistently is way better than a crazy workout every now and then.

For beginners, full-body workouts are the way to go. Why? Because they are efficient and help build whole-body strength, a rock-solid core, functional mobility, and endurance.

Sure, there's a time and place for isolation movements, but unless you're trying to compete for the next Mister Olympia title, stick to the full-body workouts. Burn more calories, don't panic if you miss a session, and focus on movements that guarantee you results.

Throw in some supersets, mix upper-body and lower-body focus, spice it up with a core day, and you've got a killer weekly routine. And by all means, respect your heart and lungs. Strength training sculpts muscles, but don't overlook cardio exercises.

Your prescription? A bare minimum of 150 minutes of moderate aerobic exercise or 75 minutes of vigorous activity per week. Try to get your heart pumping at least three times a week.

High-intensity exercises are short, explosive, and efficient sessions that sculpt lean muscle and fire up your metabolism (heart reaching 80-95% of its maximum rate): running, combat sports, powerful weightlifting, explosive plyometrics, etc. It's a combination of bursts, circuit of strength, and stamina. These exercises strengthen bones, build muscle, amp up metabolism, and elevate overall fitness.

Low-intensity exercises build endurance over longer sessions (heart reaching 40-50% of its maximum rate): calm walks, golf, yoga and pilates, easy bike rides, etc. These exercises improve cholesterol levels, lower blood pressure, and are gentle on joints, making them great for beginners. However, they require longer sessions for optimal benefits and are less effective for building bone density.

A mix of both high-intensity and low-intensity creates a balanced fitness regimen.

The best exercise? The one that aligns with your goals and health. Bodybuilding is a process, not an event. I've seen guys get pumped fast and lose it faster than slim fast.

***

The gym is great—no doubt about it. You've got dumbbells, weight machines, kettlebells, squat racks, cardio equipment—everything you need for a full workout. You've got people around you grinding and sweating. It's motivating.

But the gym also makes you lazy. The comfortable, air-conditioned environment, the machines, the lockers with the spa and all that shit... It's distracting. The gym builds dependence.

Dependence on things you don't even need to exercise and stay in shape.

You know where Arnold started working out? In the forests of Austria. No equipment. Just relentless determination.

There's something you get from training outside, or at home, with no equipment, and forcing yourself to be creative and disciplined in spite of it. That builds a habit that lasts a lifestyle. Because what will you do when the gym shuts down—for whatever reason?

No pain, no gain.

Renewal

The bloodstream reigns supreme. It's the lifeline that dispatches oxygen and nutrients to every cell—the backbone of longevity and vitality. Controlling that lifeline starts with breathing. Breath isn't just a reflex; it's the power switch, the engine, the ignition for every cell. When you breathe right, you aren't just filling your lungs—you're lighting up every inch of yourself with an electrical pulse that fuels you.

Deprive your cells of oxygen, and you're playing with fire—or rather, cancer. Look at athletes, they face fewer cancer battles than the average guy. They know the truth: oxygen is the ultimate ally.

Yet most people are sleepwalking through the very act that could save them. Breathing is automatic, thoughtless. But turn it intentional, make it mindful, and it becomes a tool of pure, unfiltered power. Breath work exercises physical, mental, and emotional healing through intentional breath control.

Most people don't know how to breathe. In America, one in three fights with cancer, but for athletes, it's one in seven. Why? Because they need to breathe well to perform well. Here's the magic ratio: inhale for one count, hold for four, exhale for two.

Exhale longer to dump toxins, and hold two to four times longer to infuse the blood with oxygen.

Don't get too focused on the logistics—make up your own ratios. Who cares? Just stick to the basics.

Stop, and take ten deep breaths, three times a day. Inhale, hold, exhale—repeat.

Respiratory muscle conditioning has many psychological physical benefits: relaxation, enhanced attention, an improved emotional state, reduced stress and anxiety, better sleep, social connectedness, and boosted self-esteem.

Revival

After you've beat your body down through intense workouts, endless workdays, or mind-numbing study marathons, it cries out for repair—something you can't afford to ignore. Enter the forces of heat and cold, nature's ancient healers, ready to revive you.

***

The cold is merciless but righteous.

Welcome discomfort, embrace the cold, and make yourself hard to kill.

In the pursuit for holistic well-being, an immersive cold plunge proves to be a powerful weapon. Beyond the initial shock, this practice unlocks a treasure trove of benefits that cascade through the body, leaving in their wake a rejuvenated sense of vitality.

Cold therapy goes back centuries, with ancient Greeks and Romans believing in its healing powers. This ain't a trend... it's been going on for a long time time.

The Vikings were some of the toughest motherfuckers to ever walk this Earth, and they fucking loved the cold—I mean, it was in their DNA. In Scandinavia, this was a way of life. They'd loosen up with intense sauna sessions, then dive straight into the nordic freezing waters like it was nothing. They believed this would amplify '*livskraft*' (life force) and give them immortality.

In the past, the healing powers of cold therapy were accepted and respected—but in modern times, they've been neglected. The wisdom passed down from ancient civilizations got lost in the shuffle of modern medicine's profit-driven agenda.

But, because we—well... not you or me, but society as a whole—have become a culture of pleasure-seekers, we forgot about these healing therapies, focusing instead on quick, easy fixes.

The real always survives. Some traditions endure, standing the test of time.

Through time and science, cold therapy has proven to be a powerful tool for recovery, with its secrets slowly unfolding through the diligent work of researchers across centuries.

Superficially, the cold tightens your skin, giving it a healthy glow and improving its overall complexion. The contraction and expansion of blood vessels boost blood flow to the skin, leaving it looking vibrant and refreshed. Cold exposure also stimulates collagen production, enhancing skin elasticity and smoothing out fine lines and wrinkles. Plus, it helps ease inflammation and puffiness, leaving you fresh and rejuvenated.

Physiologically, cold exposure activates your body's survival mechanisms. Blood vessels constrict, conserving heat by redirecting blood to vital organs. This not only eases muscle soreness—especially after intense activities—but also boosts circulation and improves your heart's efficiency in pumping oxygenated blood. [53. 54]

On a deeper level, cold therapy triggers a flood of endorphins, the body's natural mood boosters. These brain chemicals work like built-in pain relievers, lifting your spirit and dulling discomfort. [52]

Psychologically, the impact of the cold tests your mental strength. Making the decision to embrace the cold is like a mental resilience exercise. Stepping into the cold directly challenges your comfort zone, a test of your inner fortitude. As you push through the shock, something shifts inside, toughening your resolve and preparing you to face life's challenges head-on.

Chemically, the shock of the cold triggers a stress response, releasing hormones that increase alertness and focus. Simultaneously, the body produces a protein that regulates glucose levels and supercharges your metabolism. It's like flipping a switch for more energy and a turbocharged metabolism. The temporary stress induced by the cold also stimulates the endocrine system, leading to a boost in testosterone production—a shock to the system that revs up your hormonal engine. [47, 48]

At the cellular level, cold exposure stimulates the production of heat-shock proteins, which act as guardians for cells under stress, fortifying their resilience. This enhancement of cellular defence improves overall cellular health. Additionally, cold therapy activates brown adipose tissue, a type of fat that burns calories to generate heat, helping your stay lean and mean. [51]

By deliberately choosing to embrace the cold, you unlock a realm of transformative benefits, emerging from the icy waters with a renewed sense of vigor and resilience.

***

From the Nordics to the Native Americans, heat therapy has been praised by cultures all throughout history as a spiritual practice believed to develop magical powers.

It all started in caves, and with time evolved into what we have today.

Sauna therapy is about harnessing the power of heat in a confined space, warming up the body temperature, and inducing hyperthermia. In the old time, it was about spiritual revitalization—now, it's about health: elevating core temperature and inducing sweat.

Cardio health, stress relief, detoxification, metabolism boost, muscle growth, and HGH release—all from the fiery heat. That's the magic of the sauna.

Studies show that sauna therapy helps heart health, lowering blood pressure and peptides linked to heart failure. Two to three weekly sessions of fifteen minutes cuts cardiovascular mortality by forty percent. It is also associated with an increase in testosterone levels. On the flip side, while the direct impact on testosterone levels is not fully verified, repeated and extended use of hot tubs has been associated with a temporary decrease in sperm concentration—you're basically boiling your nuts! [47, 49, 50]

Starve The Body, Feed The Soul

The pursuit of enlightenment often begins on an empty stomach—the perpetual hunger that cuts through the static, pushes aside modern distractions, and brings you right to the raw edge of awareness. Fasting isn't just a trendy diet hack; it's ancient, primal. In an era long before the conveniences of modern agriculture, our ancestors adapted to cycles of feast and famine as a natural and necessary part of their existence.

From the dawn of civilization, physicians, religious leaders, and cultural figures have all embraced fasting, either for therapeutic purposes or as a testament to their beliefs.

Going back to the fifth century BCE, the Greek physician Hippocrates prescribed fasting for patients exhibiting certain symptoms of illness. This belief persisted through the centuries, with physicians advocating for the importance of fasting as a natural part of the recovery process.

And it wasn't always just about health. Fasting has been the gateway to the divine, to worlds beyond the senses. Saints and shamans, priests, and prophets—they all knew that fasting was the bridge between mortal and cosmic, a path to visions and revelations. Think of Siddhartha Gautama fasting for forty nine days before he became the Buddha, or the disciplined abstinence in Islam's Ramadan, or the Christian Lent. This isn't some half-baked shortcut to self-control; it's a holy ritual burned into the DNA of the human spirit.

The mind clears, the body purges.

Fasting isn't just about going without; it's about connecting with something bigger, stripping down to the essentials to see what's really there. When you fast, you don't just cut calories; you cut out everything that distracts, deludes, and diminishes you. And what's left? Strength, clarity, and a mind sharpened to a razor's edge, ready to face the world with nothing to hide behind but raw, unfiltered purpose.

Consistent intermittent fasting gives the digestive system a little break, but the magic happens when you push past twenty four hours.

<u>How fasting affects the body</u>

4-8 Hours

- Blood sugar drops

12-16 Hours (Intermittent fasting)

- HGH increases
- Fat burning begins

18-20 Hours

- Autophagy "self-eating" begins

26 Hours

- Autophagy increases by 300%

48 Hours

- HGH increases by 500%

54 Hours

- Insulin sensitivity increases by 500%

72 Hours

- Autophagy peaks

Fasting acts as a cognitive enhancer—like an adrenaline shot. Neurotransmitters like brain-derived neurotrophic factor (BDNF) light up, pushing your brain into a growth phase where learning accelerates and mental agility sharpens. Low BDNF levels are tied to neurodegenerative diseases like Alzheimer's and Parkinson's. [10]

And on the cellular level? Fasting triggers autophagy, the body's self-cleaning mode, where worn-out cells are dismantled, repurposed, and recycled. Old immune cells are swapped out as stem cell activity kicks in, crafting a brand-new defence force from the inside. A seventy-two-hour fast transforms your body into a regeneration machine.

Studies have concluded that, in specific cases, fasting might curb tumor growth and amplify chemotherapy's effectiveness and even lessen its brutal side effects.

Other studies have unveiled fasting's power to reshape the gut, boosting beneficial bacteria linked to a longer, healthier life. Fasting has the ability to delay disease and stretch the clock. [13, 14]

Less is more!

At Cornell University, Dr. Clive McCay doubled the lifespan of lab rats by cutting their food by half. The University of Texas pushed the idea further—keeping the same calorie intake but slashing protein for one group. The result? The low-protein group outlived the rest—what you eat matters just as much as how much. [15, 16]

Fasting is effective in reducing total cholesterol, blood pressure, triglycerides, chronic inflammation, and heart disease risk factors. Fasting also improves blood sugar control—a crucial defence against diabetes.

Fasting amplifies human growth hormone (HGH) levels naturally, fueling metabolism, muscle growth, and weight loss—no injections or special formulas. It's pure, primal chemistry, unlocking strength without forcing the body to compromise. [12]

But it doesn't stop there. There's a point in fasting where the brain gets high on its own supply, releasing endorphins and shifting to a new plane. A natural euphoria rises up as the spirit, freed from the flesh's endless demands, finds altitude. The body undergoes renewal, and the spirit finds liberation.

Fasting is the art of staying healthy, young, and hungry for life. But it's not for everyone—so practice with caution. And please, go easy when you break your fast! It's not a feast; it's a resurrection. Your stomach is empty and fragile. Start light and build your hunger back up slowly.

Sexual Transmutation

Sex can lift you up, and can bring you down. Sex is life in every sense of the word. Sex is power, and also weakness.

Energy is the currency of the universe—emotional, mental, sexual, spiritual, and a collection of frequencies, vibrations, colors, and sounds.

Everything from the inanimate to the animate pulsates with energy. We're energetic beings inhabiting an energetic reality, whether we're aware of these subtle forces or not.

You think of someone, and they call; you sense a presence before it manifests; you feel drained or energized around certain people; the full moon stirs higher emotions; an orgasm sparks a wave of ecstasy. These are the manifestations of energy.

Sexual energy is more than a primal instinct. It's life force, the genesis of creation, and the sustainer of existence. It's more than just making babies or releasing an orgasm! It's a force that, with the right intent, can be channeled toward any purpose, passion, or goals.

Sex, sexuality, and sexual energy are fundamental to your essence.

You are more than your physical form; you're a sophisticated energy infrastructure.

This design, divinely intelligent, grants you the ability to interact with universal forces. Perceive beyond the visible, attune your senses to the ethereal layers that define your existence.

Master your internal power—design your destiny.

Sexual transmutation and sublimation are alchemical processes that turn the raw, dense crude oil of sexual energy into a refined, potent elixir.

Unlock your internal power.

Alchemy

Transmute /tranz'mju:t/ : to change or alter in form, appearance, or nature and especially to a higher form. "The quest to transmute lead into gold."

Still, due to the ignorance and the distorted teachings that we endure while learning about sex, our mind fixates primarily on the physical.

Sex transmutation is the shift of the mind—from thoughts of physical expression to contemplations of different nature.

Sex is a motivator—it pushes men to excel, to succeed, and to win. Sex is one of the strongest human desires, a force that can drive men to risk life and reputation in pursuit of its satisfaction. Sex is bad when it controls you; it is good when you control it. When mastered and channeled skillfully into purpose, this motivation retains its core attributes—fueling imagination, courage, and more.

The desire for sexual expression is hardwired into your DNA. It's like a raging river. If you dam it up, it will find a way through. Ignore it, and it will find its outlet in wasted potential. But channel it—aim it with precision—and it becomes the source of your superpower.

DO YOU UNDERSTAND?

Sex is energy. Sex is fuel. And when you learn to transmute that energy, you're no longer beholden to it. You are its master.

Eliminate an animal's sex glands, and you strip away the primary source of action. A castrated bull loses its might and becomes docile. Sex alteration, whether in male or female, drains the fight and vigor from their beings. Sex glands hold the key to the force that propels action.

The desire for sex is the most powerful stimulus, igniting the mind into dynamic motion.

Emotions, not reason, direct human actions. Sex is the most potent of these emotions. When harnessed, this divine energy possesses the capacity to elevate you to higher planes of thought.

You reduce yourself to the status of lower animals when you misuse this force.

Indulging in sex is no different to substance abuse. It dissipates vital energies and obstructs creative efforts.

While other mind stimulants exist, none match the potent force of sex in driving thought vibrations. Through sex transmutation, you can attain communion with infinite intelligence and tap into the storehouse of the subconscious mind.

The mind, a creature of habit, thrives on dominating thoughts. Control, facilitated by willpower, stems from persistence and habit. By converting negative emotions into positive ones, you can master your mind—transmuting the poison into an elixir for a life.

***

How do you transmute this sexual energy?

Energy is feelings.

When we say someone's got great energy, it means we feel great around them—they're vibrating at a high frequency. Bad energy, on the other hand, is extremely tense, thick, or heavy, and you can really feel it—just like when you walk into a room where something negative just happened. You say, "You can cut the tension with a knife". This is quantum physics, not pseudoscience!

Feelings come in three forms: sensation, emotion, and intuition.

Transmutation is about changing a "lower" form of energy into a "higher" one. We start with sensation because it's the densest energy form.

Sex is like collecting "raw energy".

Grounding is about stabilizing that energy in your body—it's like learning to ride a wild horse. Pay attention to gravity. If your thoughts are running wild, gravity becomes your anchor.

Love is the secret.

Your heart is right in between your sex organs and your brain. For energy to flow from body to mind, it's got to go through the heart. An open heart means being willing to feel the emotion of love. Sex allowing love is a whole different ball game than sex blocking love. And no, you don't need to be in romantic love; it's a universal love.

With a closed heart, the energy stays trapped in the body, leading to all sorts of nasty consequences. Have you ever had sex with a closed heart? Probably felt empty or resentful afterward. But with an open heart, eros flows.

When two souls get intimate, they open up like books, sharing parts of themselves in ways words can't capture. It's raw, unfiltered, electric. The heat of the moment cracks open those channels—an energetic data highway between two people. It's a moment of surrender, where you let go of control and fall into body, mind, and raw emotion. You're not just close; you're plugged into something infinite.

Now, if you fuck with everybody and anybody, you're basically mixing and matching energies like a bad DJ. You're not just sharing physical space; you're exchanging frequencies. It's a connection thing. You wouldn't plug your phone into just any computer, would you?

Things can get messy real quick. It's like trying to juggle too many balls at once. To stay grounded, be pickier or just stick with one partner to keep your energy safe.

Life Force

Semen is life. It's the blueprint of your physical existence, whether you're male or female—you're here because of one special sperm.

Semen retention isn't magical; it's all about mental, physical, or spiritual elevation.

Here are a few interesting and convincing studies:

In 2018, researchers studied how abstaining from orgasm affects sperm. Turns out, less than a day of abstinence helps with better sperm movement. [43]

In 2003, researchers found a link between short-term abstinence and changes in testosterone levels, with a testosterone peak on day seven of abstinence. [44]

In 2001, a study uncovered elevated testosterone levels in men who held off on ejaculations for three weeks. [45]

There is a massive restorative aspect of semen retention that affects you on many different layers. So not only are you accumulating power, you are getting back to what you should be as a human male.

Semen retention is about abstaining from orgasm. For many men, the frequency at which they have sex is much lower than the one at which they masturbate, so masturbation will be the main way semen is spilled. Retention during sex is entirely different.

Sex is good—I'm just making a point here, so bear with me.

Porn, when combined with masturbation and orgasm (PMO) jacks up your cortisol levels (stress hormone), prolactin, dopamine, and norepinephrine, over saturating your neurotransmitters. This will leave you feeling dead—drained of your vital life energy. There is too much of a good thing!

Your body's highest energy priorities go towards production of semen. You should really limit ejaculation frequency because your vital life essence is lost every time you need to create semen.

Allow your brain to unwire then rewire to its "normal" state and stop producing massive volumes of neurotransmitters. You will be more focused and resilient in the face of pain. Since the pressure to create semen is no longer there, you now free up your body's internal energy resources for healing in other areas.

You also decrease prolactin and increase androgen receptor up-regulation. Prolactin is a depressant on serum testosterone utilization. The more prolactin is in the system, the less testosterone will bind to androgen receptors. Your androgen receptors are the receptors that utilize testosterone and make a man, a man. You can have all the testosterone in the world, but if they don't bind to the receptors, they will not do anything.

Masturbation and pornography deteriorate your brain and rewires it dramatically. Your prefrontal cortex (the part that is responsible for decision-making) starts getting shut down and rewired. The results from this mental destruction are an inflamed sex drive, "brain fog", lack of motivation, depression, anxiety, inability to concentrate, erectile dysfunction...

DO YOU UNDERSTAND!

Not only that, but addiction freezes you on a mental level at the time you started the addiction. So if you become addicted at fifteen, some part of you will still be psychologically fifteen years old.

Stopping PMO puts you at peace in your mind. Things that seemed boring before now become tolerable or even enjoyable. In addition, your brain will be "unfrozen". You can now start "getting on" with life and catching up with things that you missed out on. Depending on how much semen you ejaculate on a daily or weekly basis, the length of time will vary but many men start feeling more clear ninety to one hundred and eighty days in the journey.

PMO halts your progress psychologically.

Instead of trying to actually solve the problem, you look for the "easy way out" because you never grew up emotionally. There are many men who are in their late twenties or early thirties who still can't deal with people, because emotionally, they are still children. They lack masculine intent. They can't assert boundaries.

Stop it and grow the fuck up. You will become more mature, expect adult things from women, from life, and you stop living in the fantasy realm of instant gratification.

A boy escapes, a man embraces.

You bring the real "you" back to the forefront, the one that was buried beneath sexual compulsion, and you start doing what you want to do and start asserting your needs.

Freeing your spirit is the most important. The "sin" of lust destroys your soul. Imagine looking through a dirty lens. You won't see clearly. Your relationship with God, with other beings, and even the world is affected.

Experience the world in its fullness. You clean the lens of lust and start seeing people and things for who they are.

Transcendence

Sexual energy is the raw, unrelenting power of creation itself—a force that can open your heart to the ferocity of love while sending you into mystical states where time, ego, and logic dissolve like ash in a wildfire. Sex is where the ego dies, stripped bare and left to burn in the heat of infinite connection.

In moments leading to climax, the spirit's essence is reflected. Vulnerability, defencelessness, carefree abandon, and a timeless sensation envelop us.

When you let this force move through you, uniting body, mind, and spirit, you channel the creative energy of the universe itself. That kind of power demands respect. Who you share this moment with matters. Your partners leave their mark on your soul, whether the encounter lasts a night or a lifetime.

We may have evolved in our thinking and approach towards life, but casual, empty unions still pollute our spiritual space. Every sexual exchange leaves echoes in your aura. The residue of negativity, toxicity, or meaningless connection clings to you like a weight on your spirit. It dulls your brilliance.

Sexual energy is both chaotic and creative, destructive and healing. Master it and transform pain into power, wounds into wisdom, and desire into divine creativity.

Sexual Transmutation

To rise in this power, you must first purge the poison. Cleanse your spirit like you'd detox your body. Surrender to nature. Practice forgiveness—not for them, but for yourself. Sit in meditation until the chaos inside quiets, and you can hear your soul whisper.

Sexual energy is a gateway to transcendence. Respect its power, honor its purpose, and recognize that through mindful connection and ritual cleansing, this primal force can elevate you to a realm where intimacy becomes enlightenment and passion becomes purpose.

Third Eye Open

The universe is chaotic.

At any given moment, a city-sized asteroid—like the one that wiped out the dinosaurs 66 million years ago—could slam into Earth, obliterating three-quarters of life in a flash. Over the universe's billions of years, asteroids smash into planets all the time. Sure, we can spot one coming from millions of miles away, but stop it? Good fucking luck.

And what about geomagnetic storms? A powerful solar flare could potentially fry all power grids, scramble communications, and wreck GPS systems—shutting down modern civilization and sending us back to the Stone Age. Within a year, ninety percent of humanity would be gone.

Don't even get me started on WW3. Nuclear annihilation is a bigger threat now more than ever. The economy? It's being toyed with like a fucking yo-yo. Your money? It has no intrinsic value. What about the next pandemic? It's gonna come—but when?

And if you think artificial intelligence is just a shiny new tool, you're not thinking hard enough. It's already shaking the foundations of our world. No technology is foolproof—planes crash, reactors melt down, even phones blow up. AI's no different. OpenAI's o1 model showed signs of survival instincts in 2024 safety tests by Apollo Research, resisting shutdown by trying to copy itself to external servers or sabotage commands. That's chaos waiting to erupt. Worse, AI's replacing jobs faster than you can blink. Factories, offices, even creative gigs—gone. Universal basic income might keep you fed, but where the fuck do you find purpose when machines take your place? Skynet wasn't a warning; it was a prophecy.

But let's not spiral too far down the rabbit hole. This isn't about doomsday predictions or prepping for the apocalypse. It's about you. Your mind. Your ability to find calm amidst the chaos—to dim the lights when they are too bright, to lower the volume when it is too loud.

You need a control knob for this crazy world. You need to control how you react to it. You need to control it, not let it control you.

Your mind needs to be still. You are made of water, so you need to calm those waters, because the world will stir them up and create storms within you if you don't calm the fuck down.

Sit down with yourself and do nothing... think of nothing... thoughts will come, but let them pass. You are to observe, not associate; you are to witness, not participate.

Meditation might sound like something reserved for Zen masters, but it's essential to shake off the stress and walk through this chaotic world level-headed.

If stress has you feeling like you're on the edge of a skyscraper—anxiety-ridden and tense—you need to sit with yourself for a moment and find your centre. Spending a few minutes in meditation can help you to restore a bit of calm and inner peace amidst the chaos.

Liberation

Meditation liberates you from internal chaos.

Liberation is like sculpting—it's not about adding, but chipping away at what it ain't.

We're stuck in trying to define everything with words, but reality isn't a fixed, solid thing; it's an ever-changing process.

It's the undefinable, the process of the world, the way of life. Not just a road, but also a way of being—a cosmic, ever-flowing force.

Let your legs walk on their own. Liberation is not about vacating your mind but unleashing its innate intelligence without a forced grip.

Life is full of frustration, caused by our never-ending grasp. The remedy? Nirvana—not a desire, but a realization, an end to the karmic loop.

Liberation without striving, desiring not to desire.

Life's about the present; there's no past or future backstage pass. In sitting, just sit; in walking, just walk—no wobbling between opposites. No goals, no endgame. It's about the journey, not the destination.

It's the liberation from time, a dance with the eternal now. Open your eyes, see clearly, and realize that there's no time but this instant—past and future are just abstract illusions. Travel without a point, because arriving is just being dead.

***

Overlooking spirituality, meditation is really an intellectual exercise—it's like a personal project dedicated to cultivating mindfulness. The primary goal revolves around achieving a heightened state of awareness. Beyond the foundational stress relief and anxiety reduction, meditation serves as a catalyst for new perspectives, attitude changes, and a deeper way of living.

Meditation works on everyone differently—dictated by the practice you choose and the commitment you bring to it. The impatient fools, always chasing that quick fix, will mistake momentary calm for enlightenment—a placebo, not real progress. Then there are the quitters, too weak to endure the silence. Don't be a quitter!

Meditation won't solve your problems—it illuminates them, forces you to confront the raw, unfiltered truth you've been avoiding. The mental clarity it delivers is priceless, but to wield it against the demons of complex disorders or tangled dilemmas takes unrelenting discipline and brutal honesty.

But with adequate practice and the right style, the force will come.

Mindfulness—the art of living fully in the present—is the ultimate goal. It grants you the power to step back from the relentless stream of thoughts, cultivating self-awareness and the ability to observe your mind and emotions with calm detachment.

Dwelling on the past or future triggers states of stress and anxiety—mindfulness provides a pathway to liberation. By observing your thought patterns, you loosen the grip of anxious thinking, recognizing that it's the judgment of those thoughts, not the thoughts themselves, that causes anxiety. Research shows that mindfulness meditation programs targeting anxiety can significantly reduce the inflammatory response triggered by stress. And with less stress comes an abundance of benefits, including lower blood pressure. [17, 20] [37, 38, 39]

Neurodegenerative diseases are caused by the progressive loss of structure or function of neurons. While factors like genetics, age, and environment play significant roles, stress, poor thinking patterns, and a lack of mental stimulation certainly don't help the situation.

Research has shown that meditation sharpens your mind, keeping your mind young. [31, 32, 33]

It also offers relief from depression, providing peace that rivals traditional antidepressants. [18, 19, 21, 22]

Want to learn faster? Meditate. It's that simple. Focus is a like muscle, and you can strengthen it through meditation. [23, 24, 25, 26]

Meditation cultivates positive emotions, contributing to happiness and resilience in the face of challenges. Anger becomes easier to manage as emotional reactivity is defused. [40, 41]

It lifts you out of mental rigidity, sparking innovative thinking. Your decision-making? Sharper. Your logic? Clearer. [27]

With great awareness comes great self-control. You can observe cravings, addictions, and impulses without being enslaved by them. [28, 29, 30]

Meditation also improves sleep, creating the perfect environment for rest by clearing intrusive thoughts and balancing melatonin levels. [34]

Pain? It's all in your head. Whether it's chronic discomfort or distracting sensations, meditation is your brain's ultimate weapon against it. [35, 36]

Equanimity—the calm, balanced state you cultivate through regular meditation—extends beyond the practice, fostering peace in day-to-day life. Beyond the science and the data, meditation opens doors to self-reflection, self-awareness, and deep introspection, offering you a chance to truly know yourself.

Meditation isn't a replacement for therapy or medication—it's a weapon, a sharp, quiet blade that carves out space for clarity and calm. When you step onto this path, the changes in your mind send shockwaves through every corner of your life, reshaping how you see, feel, and experience the world. It's not just a practice; it's a revolution—an unstoppable force that can enrich your existence in ways no pill, no quick fix, could ever touch.

Your mind will thank you for it.

No Mud, No Lotus

I discovered myself in the darkness, surrounded by echoes of shattered dreams and unspoken agony. Pain was an uninvited guest, lingering like a venomous snake ready to strike when least expected.

They say life is a bumpy ride, but they never tell you about the potholes that will test the strength of every step you take.

Pain is not some mystical force; it's the unfiltered truth of existence, a relentless teacher that does not give a fuck about your comfort zone. It's the gut-punch that wakes you up when you're sleepwalking through your own life. Pain is the reminder that you're still alive, even when you wish you weren't.

When your world spins out of control, your dreams become nightmares, and you make your descent into darkness, pain becomes your guiding star. Instead of running from it, run to it. Walk through the fire; lean into the very thing that threatens to consume you.

Pain isn't just suffering; it forges your character. It strips away the illusions and reveals the raw essence of who you are. In those moments of suffering, you discover strength you never knew you had. It's easy to be a saint in paradise, but down here, where the air is thick with despair, pain separates the weak from the strong.

Pain is a force for change. It pushes you to the edge, daring you to leap into the unknown. When you embrace it, you find resilience in the face of adversity. You discover the grit to stand tall when the world expects you to fall. It's not about the absence of pain; it's about moving forward in spite of it. It's about getting up and keeping fighting after you've been knocked down.

They say diamonds are forged under pressure. Pain is the pressure that shapes the rough edges of your soul into something precious. It's the chisel that sculpts the masterpiece of your being. So when life hits you, don't flinch; stand tall and let the pain carve out the legend within you.

Sure, it's tempting to run from the hurt, drown it in distractions, or numb it with false comforts. But let me tell you, that's a fool's gamble. The more you run from it, the faster pain catches up. Face it head-on, acknowledge its existence, and then rise above it.

Pain is the baseline that underscores every triumph. It's the bitter truth that makes the sweet moments taste even better.

Lean into the pain, let it be your guide, and watch as it makes you hard to kill.

***

Sacrifice yourself, die and rise from the ashes like the mighty Phoenix—reborn, stronger, and unstoppable.

Turn PAIN into GAIN.

All powers are unearthed through immense pain. Bruce Wayne is only Batman because his parents were murdered.

Embrace the pain. Life is a painful journey sprinkled with tiny moments of pleasure. We are all, in essence, striving to survive—it's just that some are too comfortable to acknowledge it.

If it lies within your control, it's worth every ounce of effort and energy.

Embrace the good, the bad, and the ugly. Look in the mirror and face the reflection.

No Mud, No Lotus

"How" questions elevate the mind, propelling it to higher realms of thought and a focus on the future. On the contrary, "why" questions drag you back to the past, trapping you in the mundane. Choose your questions wisely, because they shape the course of your life. Decide what parts of your existence need a facelift or a full-on reinvention. Work on it 'till it's in your bones, 'till it's as natural as breathing. Cherish that fucked-up childhood, those dumbass mistakes, and that so-called bad environment. They're not weights around your neck— they're your secret weapons. They're the fire that'll push you to rise, make you unbreakable, and hard to kill.

No mud, no lotus. Bad times are fertilizers.

Without the chaos, the screw-ups, and the muddy waters, you wouldn't have the fire to push yourself further. You'd be sitting there, soft and complacent, basking in the glow of who you already are. But here's the truth—comfort isn't where the action is. Comfort's the enemy, the killer of ambition, the grim reaper of high-performance, self-improvement, and evolution. It's a slow, insidious killer, whispering sweet nothings in your ear, convincing you to settle into the cushy armchair of mediocrity.

So… embrace the chaos, the struggle, the suffering. Love the discomfort, 'cause that's where the real magic happens—where ambition is born, where evolution is forged. Don't shy away from the battle. Confront it, and emerge on the other side, scarred and battered, but stronger and wiser than ever before.

Pain is the ingredient. Pain is the magic.
You need to suffer.
More than you think you need.
Pain is the elixir of existence.

The Art Of Dying

"A coward dies a thousand times before his death, but the valiant taste of death but once. It seems to me most strange that men should fear, seeing that death, a necessary end, will come when it will come."

William Shakespeare

How would you feel about your life if you'd only have just a few moments left to live?

Would you be happy with where you are right now?

If this is what it is… is it enough? Are you fulfilled? Did you do everything you needed to do? Are you comfortable knowing that if you died right now, standing exactly where you are, that this would be your end?

If not, then you have work to do!

***

Every day you live is a day closer to death. This should lift you up, not bring you down.

Embrace it!

You need to find a more elegant approach to life and death.

Death should be your friend.

Death should be your teacher.

Death should be your compass.

Go where your soul shines bright. Go where time does not exist. Go where you want to die.

Death is Certain, Life is Not

Death is taboo. Nobody wants to speak about it!

We dress it up as the Grim Reaper, waiting patiently on our impending demise.

Death is really the only thing that all of us have in common. We will all eventually die! Some sooner than later. But we will all definitely die.

We avoid discussing it, causing useless suffering. The fear of death is so strong that we often prolong each other's lives, even in indecent or vegetative states, unable to confront our own inevitable fate.

Funeral directors are artists at beautifying death, investing hours in makeup and dress-up to shield us—the living—from the brutal truth… Mortality.

The soul is eternal, the body is just a vessel.

Most people spend their lives running away from death, treating it like a persistent beggar in the street, willfully blind and deaf to the footsteps of mortality tailing them. But why?

There's no thought more inspiring, exciting, or motivating than the idea of your death. It's the driving force that propels you to achieve, urging you to seize the moment.

***

From the beginning, there's one truth—we're born, and someday we'll die. That's the deal. The only unquestionable, one-hundred-percent proof certainty about life. Ironically, we spend most of our days trying to forget it.

You have been living as though death is not part of the equation, wasting precious days in unfulfilling jobs and draining relationships. Instead of expressing gratitude for the gift of life, you pursue more relentlessly, acting as if life itself is insufficient.

This is what your life has become—an endless pursuit for more, distracting you from the beauty of the present moment.

You might think immortality could be fun, but it would eventually get boring. Doing the same shit over and over again, until it all blends into monotony. Whether you're doing this or you're doing that, it all becomes repetitive.

Our time on Earth is thrilling because it's limited. The excitement lies in the fact that, at some point, it will end. That's what keeps things interesting.

Think about your death—not the funeral arrangements, but your actual exit. As your final hour approaches, how do you imagine feeling? What will you be thinking? We all die alone, but who do you want witnessing your last moments? Strangers or people you loved, people you shared memories with, people you truly connected with.

In those last moments, will you stay present, or get lost in fantasies about what lies beyond?

You should go out having fully and truly lived—sucking every drop of excitement from your time here. To die happy means leaving with the knowledge that you've infused as much light, love, and happiness into yourself and those around you as humanly possible.

You should want to die smiling. You should want to exit in absolute peace—ensuring your rest is eternal, inspiring those who witness your departure to keep living—and living well.

Death is exciting. Not because of some afterlife fantasy, but because it gives us the ultimate reason to live—and to live now. To embrace every passion, exorcise every demon, pursue every curious avenue, and dive into life every fucking day.

Living in willful ignorance of death cheats us and others out of joy. Ignoring death only brings it closer.

Death is not the enemy. It's the shadow that gives meaning to the light. You can't have one without the other. Life and death are the yin and yang of existence, and denying that truth only leads to a hollow, fear-ridden existence.

Once you accept death—stare it in the face and say, "I see you"—it loses its grip on you. Suddenly, life takes on a whole new meaning.

Death isn't the end; it's a new beginning. It's the chance to leave a mark, a legacy that echoes through time. So, why run from it? Why deny the inevitable? Embrace death, and you'll find the courage to live unapologetically.

Death has been my shadow, and I've welcomed it like an old friend. It's the whisper in my ear that says: "You're alive, so live."

So… Welcome death. Imagine what it will be like in the end. Picture life slipping away as death takes over.

How do you want to die?

***

As you finish this book, you're closer to death than when you started. Death could come at any moment. In every moment, there's a real chance your time on Earth will end. Death follows our every move.

Make no mistake: it will end. Your breath is not eternal. Your flesh will rot, surrendering to the earth, consumed by worms and time's relentless appetite. You will die, and so will everyone you love. One day, even the memory of your existence will dissolve into the void, erased without trace.

So... what now?

Live!

Live now, and live powerfully. Live with great energy, passion, and strength. Don't stop until you're so fucking satisfied with living that death seams easy.

Show up fully and enjoy the beauty of existence.

Rather than resist the relentless march of time, flow with it, turn it around and dance with death.

Possibly, you have never truly lived.

Embrace life in all its beauty and complexity.

Become, Don't Be

You are a function of the universe—a process. You are not static. You are a "verb" in the universe's abundance of processes. You are always arriving, changing, evolving, and becoming.

You are not static but dynamic. You are constantly interacting with and being changed by your surroundings.

Attune to this shift of consciousness and any mental destination seems delusional.

Projecting happiness onto symbols of victory like success, retirement, or marriage is pointless. Understanding that we never cease to become reveals the impermanence of these destinations.

Life is a process of becoming, and trying to maintain a specific state or stage is a fantasy.

Life has ups and downs, happiness will come and go. Its absence may provide perspective and sweetness to its presence.

You need the rain to appreciate the sun! You need darkness to appreciate light!

Balance the opposites! Do not judge…

It is what it is… Be okay with it.

Get out of the past, get into the present. Focus on your purpose—whatever moves you, whatever resonates with you, whatever inspires you.

Holding onto time too tightly or feeling guilt and shame over the past will cripple this process.

The past is gone. Capitalize on the possibilities of the present with optimism for the future.

Life is short if you're chasing time. Fall into the present and let time fade away.

Embrace transformation. Don't be scared!

You are not a static being. The purpose of a well-lived life involves real transformation.

You can't cheat death, but you can make yourself hard to kill. Attend to your mind, body, and soul as if your life depends on it, because it does. It won't make you immortal, but it might just give you one more day.

DO YOU UNDERSTAND?

References

[7] Intermittent fasting plus early time-restricted eating versus calorie restriction and standard care in adults at risk of type 2 diabetes (2023)

Gaskins, Xiao Tong Teong, Kai Liu, Andrew D. Vincent, Julien Bensalem, Bo Liu, Kathryn J. Hattersley, Lijun Zhao, Christine Feinle-Bisset, Timothy J. Sargeant, Gary A. Wittert, Amy T. Hutchison & Leonie K. Heilbronn

[8] Effect of intermittent fasting on circulating inflammatory markers in obesity (2022)

Andrea Mulas, Sofia Cienfuegos, Mark Ezpeleta, Shuhao Lin, Vasiliki Pavlou, and Krista A. Varady

[9] Intermittent Fasting in Cardiovascular Disorders (2019)

Bartosz Malinowski, Klaudia Zalewska, Anna Węsierska, Maya M. Sokołowska, Maciej Socha, Grzegorz Liczner, Katarzyna Pawlak-Osińska, and Michał Wiciński

[10] Effects of intermittent fasting on cognitive health and Alzheimer's disease (2023)

Mingke Guo, Xuan Wang, Yujuan Li, Ailin Luo, Yilin Zhao, Xiaoxiao Luo, and Shiyong Li

[11] Intermediate fasting and human metabolic health (2015)

Ruth E. Patterson, Gail A. Laughlin, Dorothy D. Sears, Andrea Z. LaCroix, Catherine Marinac, Linda C. Gallo, Sheri J.

Hartman, Loki Natarajan, Carolyn M. Senger, María Elena Martínez, and Adriana Villaseñor

[12] Fasting enhances growth hormone secretion and amplifies the complex rhythms of growth hormone secretion in man. (1988)

K. Y. Ho, J. D. Veldhuis, M. L. Johnson, R. Furlanetto, W. S. Evans, K. G. Alberti, M. O. Thorner

[13] The impact of intermittent fasting on gut microbiota: a systematic review of human studies (2024)

Isa Paukkonen, Elli-Noora Törrönen, Johnson Lok, Ursula Schwab, Hani El-Nezami

[14] Current Evidence and Directions for Intermittent Fasting During Cancer Chemotherapy (2021)

Kelsey Gabel, Kate Cares, Krista Varady, Vijayakrishna Gadi, Lisa Tussing-Humphreys

Intermittent fasting in the prevention and treatment of cancer (2021)

Katherine K Clifton, Cynthia X Ma, Luigi Fontana, Lindsay L Peterson

[15] The effect of retarded growth upon the length of life span and upon the ultimate body size. (1935)

C M McCay, M F Crowell, L A Maynard

[16] The Role of Hormesis in Life Extension by Caloric Restriction

Edward J. Masoro Edward J. Masoro Barshop

[17] A comparison of mindfulness-based stress reduction and an active control in modulation of neurogenic inflammation (2013)

Melissa A. Rosenkranz a, Richard J. Davidson a b c, Donal G. MacCoon a, John F. Sheridan d, Ned H. Kalin c, Antoine Lutz a.

[18] Mindfulness-Based Interventions for Anxiety and Depression (2017)

Stefan G. Hofmann, Ph.D and Angelina F. Gómez, B.A.b.

[19] Observing the Effects of Mindfulness-Based Meditation on Anxiety and Depression in Chronic Pain Patients (2015)

Kim Rod.

[20] Randomized Controlled Trial of Mindfulness Meditation for Generalized Anxiety Disorder: Effects on Anxiety and Stress Reactivity (2013)

Elizabeth A. Hoge, M.D., Eric Bui, M.D., Luana Marques, PhD, Christina A. Metcalf, B.A., Laura K. Morris, B.A., Donald J. Robinaugh, M.A, John J. Worthington, M.D., Mark H. Pollack, M.D.,and Naomi M. Simon, M.D.

[21] Meditation programs for psychological stress and well-being: a systematic review and meta-analysis (2013)

Madhav Goyal, Sonal Singh, Erica M S Sibinga, Neda F Gould, Anastasia Rowland-Seymour, Ritu Sharma, Zackary Berger, Dana Sleicher, David D Maron, Hasan M Shihab, Padmini D Ranasinghe, Shauna Linn, Shonali Saha, Eric B Bass, Jennifer A Haythornthwaite

[22] Critical Analysis of the Efficacy of Meditation Therapies for Acute and Subacute Phase Treatment of Depressive Disorders: A Systematic Review

Felipe A. Jain, M.D., Roger N. Walsh, M.D., Ph.D., Stuart J. Eisendrath, M.D., Scott Christensen, B.A., and B. Rael Cahn, M.D., Ph.D.

[23] Brief Mindfulness Meditation Improves Attention in Novices: Evidence From ERPs and Moderation by Neuroticism (2018)

Catherine J. Norris, Daniel Creem, Reuben Hendler, and Hedy Kober

[24] Meditation Effects on the Control of Involuntary Contingent Reorienting Revealed With Electroencephalographic and Behavioral Evidence (2018)

Shao-Yang Tsai, Satish Jaiswal, Chi-Fu Chang, Wei-Kuang Liang, Neil G. Muggleton, and Chi-Hung Juan

[25] On mind wandering, attention, brain networks, and meditation (2013)

Amit Sood, David T. Jones

[26] Brief, daily meditation enhances attention, memory, mood, and emotional regulation in non-experienced meditators (2018)

Julia C Basso, Alexandra McHale, Victoria Ende, Douglas J Oberlin, Wendy A Suzuki

[27] Mindful creativity: the influence of mindfulness meditation on creative thinking (2013)

Viviana Capurso, Franco Fabbro, and Cristiano Crescentini

References

[28] Integration of Transcendental Meditation into alcohol use disorder treatment (2018)

Jan Gryczynski, Robert P Schwartz, Marc J Fishman, Courtney D Nordeck, James Grant, Sanford Nidich, Stuart Rothenberg, Kevin E O'Grady

[29] A translational neuroscience perspective on mindfulness meditation as a prevention strategy (2016)

Yi-Yuan Tang, Leslie D. Leve

[30] Mindfulness-based treatment of addiction: current state of the field and envisioning the next wave of research (2018)

Eric L. Garland and Matthew O. Howard

[31] Meditation-based interventions for family caregivers of people with dementia: a review of the empirical literature (2013)

Robyn V. C. Hurley, Tom G. Patterson, Sam J. Cooley

[32] Stress, Meditation, and Alzheimer's Disease Prevention: Where The Evidence Stands (2015)

Dharma Singh Khalsa

[33] The potential effects of meditation on age-related cognitive decline: a systematic review

Tim Gard, Britta K. Hölzel, Sara W. Lazar

[34] A Randomized Controlled Trial of Mindfulness Meditation for Chronic Insomnia (2014)

Jason C. Ong, PhD, Rachel Manber, PhD, Zindel Segal, PhD, Yinglin Xia, PhD, Shauna Shapiro, PhD, James K. Wyatt, PhD.

[35] Mindfulness Meditation for Chronic Pain: Systematic Review and Meta-analysis (2017)

Lara Hilton, MPH, Susanne Hempel, PhD, Brett A. Ewing, MS, Eric Apaydin, MPP, Lea Xenakis, MPA, Sydne Newberry, PhD, Ben Colaiaco, MA, Alicia Ruelaz Maher, MD, Roberta M. Shanman, MS, Melony E. Sorbero, PhD, and Margaret A. Maglione

[36] Meditation programs for psychological stress and well-being: a systematic review and meta-analysis (2014)

Madhav Goyal, Sonal Singh, Erica M. S. Sibinga, Neda F. Gould, Anastasia Rowland-Seymour, Ritu Sharma, Zackary Berger, Dana Sleicher, David D. Maron, Hasan M Shihab, Padmini D. Ranasinghe, Shauna Linn, Shonali Saha, Eric B. Bass, Jennifer A. Haythornthwaite

[37] Investigating the effect of transcendental meditation on blood pressure: a systematic review and meta-analysis (2015)

Z. Bai, J. Chang, C. Chen, P. Li, K Yang, I. Chi

[38] Meditation can produce beneficial effects to prevent cardiovascular disease (2014)

Marcia Kiyomi Koike, Roberto Cardoso.

[39] Meditation: should a cardiologist care? (2013)

Stephen Olex, Andrew Newberg, Vincent M. Figueredo

[40] Effect of kindness-based meditation on health and well-being: a systematic review and meta-analysis (2014)

Julieta Galante, Ignacio Galante, Marie-Jet Bekkers, John Gallacher

References

[41] The interventional effects of loving-kindness meditation on positive emotions and interpersonal interactions (2015)

Xiaoli He, Wendian Shi, Xiangxiang Han, Nana Wang, Ni Zhang, and Xiaoli Wang

[43] The impact of ejaculatory abstinence on semen analysis parameters (2018)

Brent M. Hanson, Kenneth I. Aston, Tim G. Jenkins, Douglas T. Carrell, James M. Hotaling

[44] A research on the relationship between ejaculation and serum testosterone level in men (2003)

Ming Jiang, Jiang Xin, Qiang Zou, Jin-Wen Shen

[45] Endocrine response to masturbation-induced orgasm in healthy men following a 3-week sexual abstinence (2021)

M. S. Exton, T. H. Krüger, N. Bursch, P. Haake, W. Knapp, M. Schedlowski, U. Hartmann

[46] Atrazine induces complete feminization and chemical castration in male African clawed frogs Xenopus laevis (2010)

Tyrone B Hayes, Vicky Khoury, Anne Narayan, Mariam Nazir, Andrew Park, Travis Brown, Lillian Adame, Elton Chan, Daniel Buchholz, Theresa Stueve, Sherrie Gallipeau

[47] Endocrine Effects of Repeated Hot Thermal Stress and Cold Water Immersion in Young Adult Men (2021)

Robert Podstawski, Krzysztof Borysławski, Andrzej Pomianowski, Wioletta Krystkiewicz, Piotr Żurek

[48] The Effects of a Single Whole-Body Cryotherapy Exposure on Physiological, Performance, and Perceptual Responses of Professional Academy Soccer Players After Repeated Sprint Exercise (2017)

Mark Russell 1, Jack Birch, Thomas Love, Christian J Cook, Richard M Bracken, Tom Taylor, Eamon Swift, Emma Cockburn, Charlie Finn, Daniel Cunningham, Laura Wilson, Liam P Kilduff

[49] Physical activity and television watching in relation to semen quality in young men (2016)

Gaskins, A. J., Mendiola, J., Afeiche, M., Jørgensen, N., Swan, S. H., & Chavarro, J. E.

[50] Sauna bathing is associated with reduced cardiovascular mortality and improves risk prediction in men and women: a prospective cohort study. (2018)

Tanjaniina Laukkanen, Setor K. Kunutsor, Hassan Khan, Peter Willeit, Francesco Zaccardi, and Jari A. Laukkanen

[51] Temperature-acclimated brown adipose tissue modulates insulin sensitivity in humans (2014)

Lee, P., Smith, S., Linderman, J., Courville, A. B., Brychta, R. J., Dieckmann, W., & Celi, F. S.

[52] Adapted cold shower as a potential treatment for depression (2008)

Shevchuk, N. A.

[53] What are the physiological mechanisms for post-exercise cold water immersion in the recovery from prolonged endurance and intermittent exercise? (2011)

References

Ihsan, M., Watson, G., & Abbiss, C. R.

[54] The use of ice in the treatment of acute soft-tissue injury: a systematic review of randomized controlled trials. (2006)

Bleakley, C., McDonough, S., & MacAuley, D.

[55] Changes in USDA food composition data for 43 garden crops, 1950 to 1999 (2004)

Donald R Davis, Melvin D Epp, Hugh D Riordan

[56] An Alarming Decline in the Nutritional Quality of Foods: The Biggest Challenge for Future Generations' Health (2024)

Raju Lal Bhardwaj, Aabha Parashar, Hanuman Prasad Parewa, Latika Vyas

[57] Understanding the Link between Sugar and Cancer: An Examination of the Preclinical and Clinical Evidence (2022)

Margeaux Epner, Peiying Yang, Richard W Wagner, Lorenzo Cohen

[58] Attitude networks as intergroup realities: Using network-modelling to research attitude-identity relationships in polarized political contexts. (2023)

Adrian Lüders, Dino Carpentras, Michael Quayle

Life does not come to you;
you must go to life.
It's not about what you want,
but what you're willing to sacrifice for what you want.
To win you must be prepared to lose.
In anything a risk is worth everything.
Fortune favors the bold.